W9-BZE-933

CRIMINAL JUSTICE

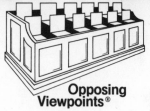

Opposing Viewpoints®

Other Books of Related Interest in the Opposing Viewpoints Series:

America's Prisons
Crime & Criminals
The Death Penalty
Social Justice

Additional Books in the Opposing Viewpoints Series:

Abortion
American Foreign Policy
The American Military
American Values
The Arms Race
Biomedical Ethics
Censorship
Central America
Chemical Dependency
Constructing a Life Philosophy
Death & Dying
Economics in America
The Environmental Crisis
Male/Female Roles
The Middle East
Nuclear War
The Political Spectrum
Problems of Africa
Science and Religion
Sexual Values
Terrorism
The Vietnam War
War and Human Nature
The Welfare State

CRIMINAL JUSTICE

Opposing Viewpoints®

David L. Bender & Bruno Leone, *Series Editors*

Bonnie Szumski, *Book Editor*

106466

OPPOSING VIEWPOINTS SERIES ®

Greenhaven Press   577 Shoreview Park Road   St. Paul, Minnesota 55126

Library of Congress Cataloging-in-Publication Data

Criminal justice.

   (Opposing viewpoints series)
   Includes bibliographies and index.
   1. Criminal justice, Administration of—United
States. I. Szumski, Bonnie, 1958-   . II. Series.
KF9223.A75C754   1987   364'.973   86-31863
ISBN 0-89908-394-3 (lib. bdg.)
ISBN 0-89908-369-2 (pbk.)

"Congress shall make no law . . . abridging the freedom of speech, or of the press."

First Amendment to the US Constitution

The basic foundation of our democracy is the first amendment guarantee of freedom of expression. The *Opposing Viewpoints Series* is dedicated to the concept of this basic freedom and the idea that it is more important to practice it than to enshrine it.

Contents

Why Consider Opposing Viewpoints?

"It is better to debate a question without settling it than to settle a question without debating it."

Joseph Joubert (1754-1824)

The Importance of Examining Opposing Viewpoints

The purpose of the Opposing Viewpoints Series, and this book in particular, is to present balanced, and often difficult to find, opposing points of view on complex and sensitive issues.

Probably the best way to become informed is to analyze the positions of those who are regarded as experts and well studied on issues. It is important to consider every variety of opinion in an attempt to determine the truth. Opinions from the mainstream of society should be examined. But also important are opinions that are considered radical, reactionary, or minority as well as those stigmatized by some other uncomplimentary label. An important lesson of history is the eventual acceptance of many unpopular and even despised opinions. The ideas of Socrates, Jesus, and Galileo are good examples of this.

Readers will approach this book with their own opinions on the issues debated within it. However, to have a good grasp of one's own viewpoint, it is necessary to understand the arguments of those with whom one disagrees. It can be said that those who do not completely understand their adversary's point of view do not fully understand their own.

A persuasive case for considering opposing viewpoints has been presented by John Stuart Mill in his work *On Liberty*. When examining controversial issues it may be helpful to reflect on this suggestion:

> The only way in which a human being can make some approach to knowing the whole of a subject, is by hearing what can be said about it by persons of every variety of opinion, and studying all modes in which it can be looked at by every character of mind. No wise man ever acquired his wisdom in any mode but this.

Analyzing Sources of Information

The Opposing Viewpoints Series includes diverse materials taken from magazines, journals, books, and newspapers, as well as statements and position papers from a wide range of individuals, organizations and governments. This broad spectrum of sources helps to develop patterns of thinking which are open to the consideration of a variety of opinions.

Pitfalls To Avoid

A pitfall to avoid in considering opposing points of view is that of regarding one's own opinion as being common sense and the most rational stance and the point of view of others as being only opinion and naturally wrong. It may be that another's opinion is correct and one's own is in error.

Another pitfall to avoid is that of closing one's mind to the opinions of those with whom one disagrees. The best way to approach a dialogue is to make one's primary purpose that of understanding the mind and arguments of the other person and not that of enlightening him or her with one's own solutions. More can be learned by listening than speaking.

It is my hope that after reading this book the reader will have a deeper understanding of the issues debated and will appreciate the complexity of even seemingly simple issues on which good and honest people disagree. This awareness is particularly important in a democratic society such as ours where people enter into public debate to determine the common good. Those with whom one disagrees should not necessarily be regarded as enemies, but perhaps simply as people who suggest different paths to a common goal.

Developing Basic Reading and Thinking Skills

In this book, carefully edited opposing viewpoints are purposely placed back to back to create a running debate; each viewpoint is preceded by a short quotation that best expresses the author's main argument. This format instantly plunges the reader into the midst of a controversial issue and greatly aids that reader in mastering the basic skill of recognizing an author's point of view.

A number of basic skills for critical thinking are practiced in the activities that appear throughout the books in the series. Some of the skills are:

Evaluating Sources of Information   The ability to choose from among alternative sources the most reliable and accurate source in relation to a given subject.

Separating Fact from Opinion   The ability to make the basic distinction between factual statements (those that can be demonstrated or verified empirically) and statements of opinion (those that are beliefs or attitudes that cannot be proved).

Identifying Stereotypes   The ability to identify oversimplified, exaggerated descriptions (favorable or unfavorable) about people and insulting statements about racial, religious or national groups, based upon misinformation or lack of information.

Recognizing Ethnocentrism   The ability to recognize attitudes or opinions that express the view that one's own race, culture, or group is inherently superior, or those attitudes that judge another culture or group in terms of one's own.

It is important to consider opposing viewpoints and equally important to be able to critically analyze those viewpoints. The activities in this book are designed to help the reader master these thinking skills. Statements are taken from the book's viewpoints and the reader is asked to analyze them. This technique aids the reader in developing skills that not only can be applied to the viewpoints in this book, but also to situations where opinionated spokespersons comment on controversial issues. Although the activities are helpful to the solitary reader, they are most useful when the reader can benefit from the interaction of group discussion.

Using this book and others in the series should help readers develop basic reading and thinking skills. These skills should improve the reader's ability to understand what they read. Readers should be better able to separate fact from opinion, substance from rhetoric and become better consumers of information in our media-centered culture.

This volume of the Opposing Viewpoints Series does not advocate a particular point of view. Quite the contrary! The very nature of the book leaves it to the reader to formulate the opinions he or she finds most suitable. My purpose as publisher is to see that this is made possible by offering a wide range of viewpoints which are fairly presented.

David L. Bender
Publisher

Introduction

"Better that many guilty shall go free rather than one innocent should suffer."

John Adams

The protection of those accused of crime has been of fundamental importance since the founding of the United States. The idea that allowing even the guilty to go free if it may protect one innocent person from conviction is regarded by many as a high ideal for which our criminal justice system must continually strive. Concurrently, a growing number of people believe that the victim of crime is sacrificed to this ideal. It is the rights of these victims, critics of the system argue, that must be of paramount consideration.

Concern for the rights of the victim has been translated into legal action in many states. Victims' legal rights have been expanded to include the right to be kept informed of all proceedings regarding their case, including preliminary hearings, plea bargaining efforts, and police investigations. Many states have established victim compensation programs, and, if the accused is convicted, some states allow the victim to participate in the parole hearings. Most controversially, the right to be present and testify at the trial has been enlarged to include the family members of murder victims, even when they were not witnesses to the crime. Typically, they testify to the extreme trauma the murder has caused their family in an attempt to plead with the court to bring justice for the family member's death.

These changes have altered the way police, lawyers, judges, and others in the criminal justice system view both the victim and the accused. While this shift in focus from the accused to the victim is heralded as a much-needed improvement by many, others worry that it will greatly diminish the rights of the accused. After all, the myriad of legal rights the accused now have at their disposal were not granted readily, but were fought for and won because many people perceived a need for such reforms. Laws like *Miranda*, in which the accused must be informed of his or her rights, are a good example. *Miranda*'s original intent was to deter and control police power by limiting unauthorized searches and interrogations. Other rights, like plea bargaining, the right to appeal a conviction, and the right to be represented by an attorney

13

even if one cannot afford one, are guarantees many people in our society applaud. However, there have always been those who criticize these protections as excessive and who argue that they allow hardened criminals to manipulate the system and escape punishment. This view seems to be gathering momentum as the victim continues gaining public sympathy and judicial support.

Whether or not the victim's increased role is positive, it represents a major shift from John Adams' ideal—a distanced and rational system of justice—to one where personal emotions like sympathy, anger, and even vengeance come into play. Will a murdered child's mother testifying before the court have such impact upon the jury that the jury will ignore the evidence? Is the courtroom becoming a battleground, where the jury is asked to take retribution and exact a type of tribal justice rather than base its decision on the facts and presentation of the case itself?

Throughout *Criminal Justice: Opposing Viewpoints* the rights of the victim and the accused appear in continual conflict. The five topics debated are: Is the Criminal Justice System Fair? Is the Litigation Crisis Destroying the Legal System? Do the Rights of the Accused Undermine the Criminal Justice System? Should the Criminal Justice System Enforce Crime Victims' Rights? Are Lawyers Ethical? While readers are drawn into the controversies debated in this book, the question of how to ensure justice for the accused will remain a perpetual problem.

1 CHAPTER

Is the Criminal Justice System Fair?

CRIMINAL
JUSTICE

"Wicked people exist. Nothing avails except to set them apart from innocent people."

The Criminal Justice System Should Focus on Punishment

James Q. Wilson

James Q. Wilson is Harry Lee Shattuck Professor of Government at Harvard University and a well-respected writer on criminal justice issues. He has served on various presidential task forces and national advisory commissions on crime, law enforcement, and drug abuse prevention. In the following viewpoint, Professor Wilson argues that the criminal justice system should focus on making sanctions against criminals more effective. Focusing on things beyond its control like poverty, racism, and inequity will not alleviate crime, he believes.

As you read, consider the following questions:

1. Why does the author argue that increasing job opportunities will not eliminate crime?
2. What are the "perverse incentives" that plague the criminal justice system, according to the author?
3. Why does Wilson argue that criminal justice resources must focus on deterrence and justice?

If we are to make the best and sanest use of our laws and liberties, we must first adopt a sober view of man and his institutions that would permit reasonable things to be accomplished, foolish things abandoned, and utopian things forgotten. A sober view of man requires a modest definition of progress. A 20 percent reduction in the number of robberies would still leave us with the highest robbery rate of almost any Western nation but would prevent over one hundred thousand robberies. A small gain for society, a large one for the would-be victims. But even this gain is unlikely if we do not think clearly about crime and public policy.

The quest for the causes of crime is an intellectually stimulating, though, thus far, rather confusing, endeavor. To the extent we have learned anything at all, we have learned that the factors in our lives and history that most powerfully influence the crime rate—our commitment to liberty, our general prosperity, our childrearing methods, our popular values—are precisely the factors that are hardest or riskiest to change. Those things that can more easily and safely be changed—the behavior of the police, the organization of neighborhoods, the management of the criminal justice system, the sentences imposed by courts—are the things that have only limited influence on the crime rate.

If the things we can measure and manipulate had a large effect on the crime rate, then those effects would by now be evident in our statistical studies and police experiments. If crime were easily deterred by changes in the certainty or severity of sanctions, then our equations would probably have detected such effects in ways that overcome the criticisms now made of such studies. If giving jobs to ex-offenders and school dropouts readily prevented crime, the results of the Manpower Demonstration Research Corporation experiments would not have been so disappointing. If new police patrol techniques made a large and demonstrable difference, those techniques would have been identified.

Yearning for the Good Old Days

In a sense, the radical critics of American society are correct: if you wish to make a big difference in crime, you must make fundamental changes in society. But they are right only in that sense, for what they propose to put in place of existing institutions, to the extent they propose anything at all except angry rhetoric, would probably make us yearn for the good old days when our crime rate was higher but our freedoms were intact. Indeed, some versions of the radical doctrine would leave us yearning for the good old days when not only were our freedoms intact, but our crime rate was lower.

I realize that some people, not at all radical, find it difficult to accept the notion that if we are to think seriously about crime, we ought to think about crime and not about poverty, unemployment, or racism. Such persons should bear two things in mind. The first is that there is not contradiction between taking crime seriously and taking poverty (or other social disadvantages) seriously. There is no need to choose. Quite the contrary; to the extent our efforts to measure the relationships among crime, wealth, and sanctions can be said to teach any lessons at all, it is that raising the costs of crime while leaving the benefits of noncrime untouched may be as shortsighted as raising the benefits of noncrime while leaving the costs of crime unchanged. Anticrime policies are less likely to succeed if there are no reasonable alternatives to crime; by the same token, employment programs may be less likely to succeed if there are attractive criminal alternatives to working. If legitimate opportunities for work are unavailable, some people may turn to crime, but if criminal opportunities are profitable, some persons will not take the legitimate jobs that exist.

Crime Does Not Pay

Currently, imprisonment is the only thing we have to demonstrate the cost of crime, and we must use it with greater consistency. Granted, the rate of recidivism for people released from prison can be argued as strong proof that correctional institutions do not correct. But at least prisons shift the locus of crime from innocent people on the street to fellow criminals behind bars.

I believe that without a solid and relatively uniform reaction on the part of the sentencing bench, the criminals are bound to win. Sentencing *must* prove to the public at large that crime does not pay.

Charles L. Weltner, *Atlanta Weekly,* May 2, 1982.

Some persons may believe that if legitimate jobs are made absolutely more attractive than stealing, stealing will decline even without any increase in penalties for it. That may be true provided there is no practical limit on the amount that can be paid in wages. Since the average "take" from a burglary or mugging is quite small, it would seem easy to make the income from a job exceed the income from crime. But this neglects the advantages of a criminal income: one works at crime at one's convenience, enjoys the esteem of colleagues who think a "straight" job is stupid and skill at stealing is commendable, looks forward to the occasional "big score" that may make further work unnecessary for weeks, and relishes the risk and adventure associated with theft.

The money value of all these benefits (that is, what one who is not shocked by crime would want in cash to forego crime) is hard to estimate but is almost certainly far larger than either public or private employers could offer to unskilled or semiskilled young workers. The only alternative for society is to so increase the risks of theft that its value is depreciated below what society can afford to pay in legal wages, and then take whatever steps are necessary to insure that those legal wages are available.

Poor People and Crime

The desire to reduce crime is the worst possible reason for reducing poverty. Most poor persons are not criminals; many either are retired or have regular jobs and lead conventional family lives. The elderly, the working poor, and the willing-to-work poor could benefit greatly from economic conditions and government programs that enhance their incomes without there being the slightest reduction in crime (indeed, if the experience of the 1960s is any guide, there might well be, through no fault of most beneficiaries, an increase in crime). Reducing poverty and breaking up the ghettoes are desirable policies in their own right, whatever their effects on crime. It is the duty of government to devise other measures to cope with crime, not only to permit antipoverty programs to succeed without unfair competition from criminal opportunities, but also to insure that such programs do not inadvertently shift the costs of progress, in terms of higher crime rates, onto innocent parties, not the least of whom are the poor themselves.

Moral Horror

One cannot press this economic reasoning too far. Some persons will commit crimes whatever the risks; indeed, for some, the greater the risk the greater the thrill, while others (the alcoholic wife beater, for example) are only dimly aware that there are any risks. But more important than the insensitivity of certain criminals to changes in risks and benefits is the impropriety of casting the crime problem wholly in terms of a utilitarian calculus. The most serious offenses are crimes not simply because society finds them inconvenient, but because it regards them with moral horror. To steal, to rape, to rob, to assault—these acts are destructive of the very possibility of society and affronts to the humanity of their victims. Parents do not instruct their children to be law abiding merely by pointing to the risks of being caught, but by explaining that these acts are wrong whether or not one is caught. I conjecture that those parents who simply warn their offspring about the risks of crime produce a disproportionate number of young persons willing to take those risks.

Even the deterrent capacity of the criminal justice system depends in no small part on its ability to evoke sentiments of shame in the accused. If all it evoked were a sense of being unlucky, crime rates would be even higher. James Fitzjames Stephens makes the point by analogy. To what extent, he asks, would a man be deterred from theft by the knowledge that by committing it he was exposing himself to one chance in fifty of catching a serious but not fatal illness—say, a bad fever? Rather little, we would imagine—indeed, all of us regularly take risks as great or greater than that: when we drive after drinking, when we smoke cigarettes, when we go hunting in the woods. The criminal sanction, Stephens concludes, "operates not only on the fears of criminals. [A] great part of the general detestation of crime . . . arises from the fact that the commission of offenses is associated . . . with the solemn and deliberate infliction of punishment wherever crime is proved."

Stigmatizing the Criminal

Much is made today of the fact that the criminal justice system "stigmatizes" those caught up in it, and thus unfairly marks such persons and perhaps even furthers their criminal careers by "label-

"Don't blame me — I'm simply a victim of our permissive society."

© Uluschak/Rothco

ing" them as criminals. Whether the labeling process operates in this way is as yet unproved, but it would indeed be unfortunate if society treated a convicted offender in such a way that he had no reasonable alternative but to make crime a career. To prevent this, society should insure that one can "pay one's debt" without suffering permanent loss of civil rights, the continuing and pointless indignity of parole supervision, and the frustration of being unable to find a job. But doing these things is very different from eliminating the "stigma" from crime. To destigmatize crime would be to lift from it the weight of moral judgment and to make crime simply a particular occupation or avocation which society has chosen to reward less (or perhaps more!) than other pursuits. If there is no stigma attached to an activity, then society has no business making it a crime. Indeed, before the invention of the prison in the late eighteenth and early nineteenth centuries, the stigma attached to criminals was the major deterrent to and principal form of protection from criminal activity. The purpose of the criminal justice system is not to expose would-be criminals to a lottery in which they either win or lose, but to expose them in addition and more importantly to the solemn condemnation of the community should they yield to temptation.

Marginal Improvements

If we grant that it is proper to try to improve the criminal justice system without apologizing for the fact that those efforts do not attack the "root causes" of crime, the next thing to remember is that we are seeking, at best, marginal improvements that can only be discovered through patient trial-and-error accompanied by hardheaded and objective evaluations.

There are, we now know, certain things we can change in accordance with our intentions, and certain ones we cannot. We cannot alter the number of juveniles who first experiment with minor crimes. We apparently cannot lower the overall recidivism rate, though within reason we should keep trying. We are not yet certain whether we can increase significantly the police apprehension rate. We may be able to change the teenage unemployment rate, though we have learned by painful trial-and-error that doing this is much more difficult than once supposed. We can probably reduce the time it takes to bring an arrested person to trial, even though we have as yet made few serious efforts to do so. We can certainly reduce any arbitrary exercise of prosecutorial discretion over whom to charge and whom to release, and we can most definitely stop pretending that judges know, any better than the rest of us, how to provide "individualized justice." We can confine a larger proportion of the serious and repeat offenders and fewer of the common drunks and truant children. We know that confining criminals prevents them from harming society, and we have grounds for suspecting that some would-be criminals can be deterred by the confinement of others.

Above all, we can try to learn more about what works and, in the process, abandon our ideological preconceptions about what ought to work. This is advice, not simply or even primarily to government—for governments are run by men and women who are under irresistible pressures to pretend they know more than they do—but to my colleagues: academics, theoreticians, writers, advisers. We may feel ourselves under pressure to pretend we know things, but we are also under a positive obligation to admit what we do not know and to avoid cant and sloganizing. . . .

Perverse Incentives

The entire criminal justice system, from citizen to judge, is governed by perverse incentives. Though many of its members agree on what they wish to achieve, the incentives faced by each member acting individually directs him or her to act in ways inconsistent with what is implied by that agreement.

In evidence of this, consider the following. Police officers want to arrest serious offenders—they are "good collars"—but making such arrests in ways that lead to conviction is difficult. Those convictions that are obtained are usually the result of the efforts of a small minority of all officers. Arrests that stand up in court tend to involve stranger-to-stranger crimes, to occur soon after the crime, and to be accompanied by physical evidence or eyewitness testimony. The officers who look hard for the perpetrators of stranger-to-stranger crimes, who gather physical evidence, and who carefully interview victims and potential witnesses are a small minority of all officers. . . .

Prosecutors also behave in many cases in ways inconsistent with a crime-control objective. In the 1960s, many of them took cases to court more or less in the order in which the arrests had been made. Then they began to assign higher priority to grave offenses. While an improvement, this still resulted in resources being concentrated on persons who had committed serious offenses, rather than on high-rate offenders. . . . These are not necessarily the same persons. By the late 1970s, many career criminal programs had become quite sophisticated: they gave highest priority to grave offenses and to offenders with long or serious records. But even now, many jurisdictions limit the selection of cases to persons with serious adult records, ignoring the high predictive value of the juvenile record and the drug-abuse history. Some prosecutors will concentrate their follow-up investigations on persons who have committed serious crimes and neglect the crime-control value of investigating suspected high-rate offenders who may have been caught for a nonserious offense.

Judges must manage a crowded docket, dispose of cases quickly, and make decisions under uncertainty. Some are also eager to minimize their chances of being reversed on appeal. These managerial concerns, while quite understandable, often get in the way of trying to use the court hearing as a means of establishing who is and who is not a high-rate offender and of allowing such distinctions, as well as the facts about the gravity of the case, to shape the sentence.

Not Even a System

To the extent the incentives operating in the criminal justice system have perverse and largely unintended effects, it is not clear what can be done about it. The "system" is not, as so many have remarked, in fact a system—that is, a set of consciously coordinated activities. And given the importance we properly attach to having an independent judiciary and to guaranteeing, even at some cost in crime control, the rights of accused by means of the adversarial process, there is no way the various institutions can be made into a true system. The improvements that can be made are all at the margin and require patient effort and an attention to detail. Sometimes a modest leap forward is possible, as when prosecutors began using computers to keep track of their cases and to learn about the characteristics of the defendants, or when legislators began experimenting with various kinds of sentencing guidelines. But mostly, progress requires dull, unrewarding work in the trenches. There is no magic bullet. . . .

We Cannot Forget

For most of us, the criminal justice system is intended for the other fellow, and since the other fellow is thought to be wicked, we can easily justify to ourselves a pinch-penny attitude toward the system. It is, after all, not designed to help us but to hurt him. If it is unpleasant, congested, and cumbersome, it is probably only what those who are caught up in its toils deserve. What we forget is that the more unpleasant the prisons, the less likely judges will be to send people to them; the more congested the prosecutor's office, the less likely that office will be to sort out, carefully, the serious and high-rate offender from the run-of-the-mill and low-rate offender; the more cumbersome the procedures, the less likely we and our neighbors will be to take the trouble of reporting crimes, making statements, and testifying in court.

Wicked people exist. Nothing avails except to set them apart from innocent people. And many people, neither wicked nor innocent, but watchful, dissembling, and calculating of their chances, ponder our reaction to wickedness as a clue to what they might profitably do. Our actions speak louder than our words.

"The criminal justice system focuses moral condemnation on individuals and deflects it away from the social order that may have. . . pushed him or her to the brink of crime."

The Criminal Justice System Should Focus on Social Inequity

Jeffrey H. Reiman

Jeffrey H. Reiman is a faculty member of the American University's School of Justice in Washington, DC. In the following viewpoint, excerpted from his book, *The Rich Get Richer and the Poor Get Prison*, Reiman contends that the criminal justice system has an economic bias: the system punishes crimes such as muggings and murder, which are primarily committed by the poor. He believes the real criminal activity is committed by the wealthy against the poor, and it is the roots of this social inequity that the criminal justice system must attack.

As you read, consider the following questions:

1. What mistake does Reiman believe the criminal justice system makes when it focuses on individual responsibility for crime?
2. Why does the author believe the criminal justice system is in itself criminal?

Reprinted with permission of Macmillan Publishing Company from *The Rich Get Richer and the Poor Get Prison* by Jeffrey H. Reiman. New York: Macmillan Publishing Company, 1984.

Any criminal justice system like ours conveys a subtle, yet powerful message in support of established institutions. It does this for two interconnected reasons: first, because it concentrates on *individual* wrongdoers. This means that *it diverts our attention away from our institutions, away from consideration of whether our institutions themselves are wrong or unjust or indeed "criminal."*

Second, the criminal law is put forth as the *minimum neutral ground rules* for any social living. We are taught that no society can exist without rules against theft and violence, and thus the criminal law is put forth as politically neutral, as the minimum requirements for *any* society, as the minimum obligations that any individual owes his fellows to make social life of any decent sort possible. Thus, it not only diverts our attention away from the possible injustice of our social institutions, but *the criminal law bestows upon those institutions the mantle of its own neutrality.* Since the criminal law protects the established institutions (e.g., the prevailing economic arrangements are protected by laws against theft, etc.), attacks on those established institutions become equivalent to violations of the minimum requirements for any social life at all. In effect, the criminal law enshrines the established institutions as equivalent to the minimum requirements for *any* decent social existence—and it brands the individual who attacks those institutions as one who has declared war on *all* organized society and who must therefore be met with the weapons of war.

The Evils of the Social Order

This is the powerful magic of criminal justice. By virtue of its focus on *individual* criminals, it diverts us from the evils of the *social* order. By virtue of its presumed neutrality, it transforms the established social (and economic) order from being merely *one* form of society open to critical comparison with others into *the* conditions of *any* social order and thus immune from criticism. Let us look more closely at this process.

What is the effect of focusing on individual guilt? Not only does this divert our attention from the possible evils in our institutions, but it puts forth half the problem of justice as if it were the *whole* problem. To focus on individual guilt is to ask whether or not the individual citizen has fulfilled his obligations to his fellow citizens. *It is to look away from the issue of whether his fellow citizens have fulfilled their obligations to him.* To look only at individual responsibility is to look away from social responsibility. To look only at individual criminality is to close one's eyes to social injustice and to close one's ears to the question of whether our social institutions have exploited or violated the individual. *Justice*

25

is a two-way street—but criminal justice is a one-way street. Individuals owe obligations to their fellow citizens because their fellow citizens owe obligations to them. Criminal justice focuses on the first and looks away from the second. *Thus, by focusing on individual responsibility for crime, the criminal justice system literally acquits the existing social order of any charge of injustice!*

Criminality Is Defined by Circumstances

This is an extremely important bit of ideological alchemy. It stems from the fact that the same act can be criminal or not, unjust or just, depending on the conditions in which it takes place. Killing someone is ordinarily a crime. But if it is in self-defense or to stop a deadly crime, it is not. Taking property by force is usually a crime. But if the taking is just retrieving what has been stolen, then no crime has been committed. Acts of violence are ordinarily crimes. But if the violence is provoked by the threat of violence or by oppressive conditions, then, like the Boston Tea Party, what might ordinarily be called criminal is celebrated as just. This means that when we call an act a crime *we are also making an implicit judgment about the conditions in response to which it takes place.* When we call an act a crime, we are saying that the conditions in which it occurs are not themselves criminal or deadly or oppressive or so unjust as to make an extreme response reasonable or justified, that is, to make such a response noncriminal. This means that when the system holds an individual responsible for a crime, *it implicitly conveys the message that the*

"Fetch me the law for the rich, will you?"

social conditions in which the crime occurred are not responsible for the crime, that they are not so unjust as to make a violent response to them excusable. . . .

The criminal justice system focuses moral condemnation on individuals and deflects it away from the social order that may have either violated the individual's rights or dignity or literally pushed him or her to the brink of crime. This not only serves to carry the message that our social institutions are not in need of fundamental questioning, but it further suggests that the justice of our institutions is obvious, not to be doubted. . . .

Taking Society Off the Hook

Not only does the criminal justice system acquit the social order of any charge of injustice, it specifically cloaks the society's own crime-producing tendencies. I have already observed that by blaming the individual for a crime, the society is acquitted of the charge of injustice. I would like to go further now and argue that by blaming the individual for a crime, the society is acquitted of the charge of *complicity* in that crime. This is a point worth developing, since many observers have maintained that modern competitive societies such as our own have structural features that tend to generate crime. Thus, holding the individual responsible for his or her crime serves the function of taking the rest of society off the hook for their role in sustaining and benefiting from social arrangements that produce crime. . . .

A criminal justice system that functions like ours—that imposes its penalties on the poor and not equally on all who threaten society, that does not protect us against threats to our lives and possessions equal to or graver than those presently defined as "crimes," and that fails even to do those things that could better protect us against the crimes of the poor—*is morally no better than the criminality it claims to fight.* . . .

The argument that follows will be set forth in dialogue form, since this is the form closest to the way we argue among (and within) ourselves and thus is most accessible and most easily understood. . . .

A criminal justice system serves justice to the extent that it protects equally the interests and rights of all and to the extent that it punishes equally all who endanger these interests or violate these rights. To the extent that it veers from these goals, the criminal justice system is guilty of the same sacrificing of the interests of some for the benefit of others that it exists to combat. It is therefore, morally speaking, guilty of crime.

The experience of the twentieth century has taught us that we should not take for granted that every legal system is a system of justice. Hitler's Germany and Stalin's Russia, as well as contemporary South Africa, are testimony to the fact that what is put forth as law may well be outrageously unjust. . . . We can

27

no longer uncritically take for granted that our own legal order is just merely because it is legal. We must subject it to the moral test of whether it serves and protects the interests of all to make sure that it is not injustice disguised as justice, criminality wearing the mask of law. . . .

Let us now join the dialogue between the Critic and the Defender of the Present Legal Order. . . .

A Legal System Examined

Defender: See here, Critic, I've been listening quite patiently to you and I'm willing to agree to much of what you've said so far, but now I think you are letting your emotions get the best of you. I admit that our criminal justice system is far from perfect. I admit it may even be in need of a major overhaul. But to call it *criminal* is either just rhetoric or—if you mean it literally—confusion. A crime is a violation of the law. A legal system may be unjust, but to call it "criminal" is to ask for confusion, since a legal system can't violate the law—it is the law!

Who Is the Real Mugger?

For a variety of complex reasons, our society does not ask itself, "How do so many young people become mindlessly antisocial and, at times, self-destructive?" A painfully disturbing answer to this core question is that "mugged communities," "mugged neighborhoods" and, probably most important, "mugged schools" spawn urban "muggers."

Given this fact, a more severe criminal-justice system, more prisons and more citizen shootings will not solve the problem of urban crime.

These are selective forms of anger directed toward the visible "muggers." The educationally rejected and despised "muggers"—the pool of the unemployed and unemployable from which they come—will increase in numbers, defiance and venom. Not able to express their frustrations in words, their indignation takes the form of more crime. They now riot as individuals rather than as a mob. Having been robbed of the minimum self-esteem essential to their humanity, they have nothing to lose. No one offers them financial support for their lawless behavior. . . . They reject the values of a hypocritical society that demands that they act passively human even as their humanity is being systematically destroyed.

Kenneth B. Clark, *The New York Times,* January 14, 1985.

Critic: How foolish do you think I am? Surely you don't take me to be saying that the legal system is criminal in the sense of breaking the law.

Defender: Then say what you mean. If I'm confused, it's because

28

your argument leads to confusion. . . .

Critic: The criminal justice system is *morally indistinguishable from criminality*. That is, its use of force is morally wrong for the same reasons that make the criminal's use of force morally wrong. And what is morally indistinguishable from criminality *is* essentially criminal in every respect other than the technical one of being a violation of the criminal law.

Defender: A mere technicality, is it? I suppose I'm splitting hairs to point out that a crime is a violation of the law.

Critic: You're not splitting hairs, but you are missing an important point. Crime is morally wrong because it uses force in ways that hurt people without moral justification and because it uses the threat of force to make people do what they might not otherwise freely choose to do. Now the criminal justice system also uses force in ways that hurt people. . . .

Defender: You mean the use of force to arrest suspects or to confine convicts?

Critic: Yes. But also it uses the threat of force to limit the freedom of just about everyone else.

Making the Public Obey

Defender: Here I take it that you are referring to the fact that the system threatens punishment as a way of forcing people to comply with the criminal law.

Critic: Right again. And this means not only complying with law but putting up with the social and economic arrangements that the law protects. Just as the criminal law limits the ways in which homosexuals express their sexual desires, so it limits the ways in which the poor can alleviate the miseries of poverty or the powerless can gain more control over their lives. For instance, we've seen that the system allows harmful business practices such as pollution and inadequate occupational safety to exist. Now if the victims of these practices took action in their own self-defense against these practices, they would come up against the very property rights that the criminal justice system protects. But this means that by enforcing laws against theft and assault and the rest, *the criminal justice system is using force in ways that protect those harmful practices*. All of which means that the criminal justice system uses force in ways that directly produce considerable suffering, for example, the suffering of those who languish in prison cells or of those who must seriously limit their freedom in fear of imprisonment—and it uses force in ways that indirectly produce considerable suffering—for example, the suffering of those who receive the short end of the stick in the economic system, which the criminal justice system protects with force and the threat of force. . . .

Defender: You accept that most if not all the people who end up in prison are probably guilty of the crime or crimes that got them there.

Critic: It's hard to know these things with certainty, but I start from the assumption that those people did commit the acts that they were sentenced for and that they are *legally* guilty of those crimes. So?

Defender: So? So that's the difference. The victims of criminal force are innocent, but the victims of the force used by the criminal justice system are not at all innocent. So even if the system functions unjustly or ineffectively, as long as it uses force against people who have done wrong, it is morally different from crime. Suppose you're right that the system punishes some killers and not others. *We* may think it is unjust that the poor guy who shoots his neighbor goes to prison, while the executive responsible for deadly occupational hazards goes free. But that poor murderer can't complain about his imprisonment. *He* can't cry injustice, since, after all, he did kill someone and deserves punishment regardless of what happens to anyone else. I think this is why the criminal justice system may be accused of exercising force unjustly *but not criminally*—this is why I think your argument rests on a confusion. The system may be unjust and it may be ineffective in protecting us, but the objects of its force are not innocent victims. This is the moral difference between the criminal justice system and criminality.

Critic: I admit that some of the "victims" of the criminal justice system get what they deserve. But I think it is a mistake to think that the only victims of criminal justice policy are the people who get locked up. The criminal justice system is responsible for the victims of the acts that it doesn't use force to prevent. Since it is *the* institution that uses force to prohibit harmful acts, what it doesn't prohibit, *it permits*. Indeed, since it is the *only* institution allowed to use force, what it permits, *it protects*. The criminal justice system has many victims, and most of them are clearly innocent.

Victims of the System

Defender: Who are the innocent victims of criminal justice?

Critic: Well, first, and least controversially, there are the *millions* of citizens who fork over more than $25 billion a year (on pain of imprisonment) in taxes to pay for the false illusion of protection and justice. *This is robbery in the name of criminal justice.* Then there are the hundreds of thousands of citizens who are killed or injured by safety hazards and all the other acts that the system either winks at or closes its eyes to entirely. These people are victimized not merely because the system neglects to use force to protect them but even more so because the system uses force to protect the wealth and power of those who harm them. Add to them the thousands who are victimized by the crimes of heroin addicts and

30

of ex-convicts who can't get a decent job and by the crimes that are facilitated and intensified by the availability of guns. *An entire FBI Index of property "crimes" and violent "crimes" results from criminal justice policy.* And the victims are innocent.

Innocent Criminals?

Defender: And the criminals in prison—are they also innocent victims?

Critic: All those who are either punished or live in fear of punishment for *victimless crimes*, that is, for acts that harm no one against his or her will, those who are punished for using marijuana or heroin, for prostitution or homosexual behavior and the like are innocent victims of the criminal justice system.

Defender: What of those who are punished for crimes with victims?

Critic: I would say that for many of them, their moral guilt is questionable, and to that extent they are victimized by the system.

Defender: Before, you said that you believe that most of those now serving jail or prison sentences are guilty of the crimes for which they were convicted.

Critic: I believe that most are *legally* guilty. I think the extent of their *moral* guilt is questionable. So many of those in our prisons are poor that it seems reasonable to doubt that they would have committed the crimes that got them in prison if they had not suffered the disabilities and disadvantages of poverty. If this is so, who is morally responsible for the crimes of the poor? The poor who didn't choose their poverty or the affluent who choose to do little or nothing to rectify it? . . . There is reason to believe that a society like ours provokes crime in all economic classes, although most intensely in the lowest classes. If this is so, can you be so sure that the criminals punished by the system are not in a more profound sense really innocent victims of the system, at least in the sense that they are not morally responsible for the social conditions that have made crime such a reasonable and tempting option for them?

Defender: I think you are being a bit maudlin about criminals. Many of them are pretty nasty, not at all as innocent as you picture them.

Critic: I knew you would say that. But I have no illusions about those criminals. I don't doubt that many are dangerous and nasty and that we need to be protected against them. This, however, shouldn't be used as an excuse for ignoring the social sources of their nastiness. And if those sources are to be found in the poverty our society allows, in the selfishness our society encourages, and in the institutions our criminal justice system protects, then there is a profound sense in which our criminals are our victims. The punishment we heap upon them is just a continuation of the pains we have allowed them to suffer since birth, for no fault of their own.

Defender: Poverty is no excuse for hurting other people—certainly not other poor people.

Critic: Look, I agree with you. My point is not that all criminals are innocent but rather that the moral guilt of many criminals is less because of the social conditions that are part of their existence. Some may well be morally guilty of their crimes but for others, there is reason to believe that their guilt is at least shared by the society that allows crime-producing conditions to flourish. My point is that if you add to these all the victims of the system's action and inaction who are clearly innocent, the inescapable conclusion is that of all the hundreds of thousands of victims of our criminal justice policies and practices, many are clearly innocent, many are of questionable guilt, and a small fraction of the total are really getting what they deserve. *This is enough, I think, to make the case that the criminal justice system is morally no better than crime.* That the system is more *criminal* than *just.*

"I am unalterably opposed to legal loopholes which permit hardened, vicious criminals with long records of serious infractions to escape just and proper punishment."

The Criminal Justice System Favors Offenders

Charles L. Gould

Charles L. Gould worked on newspapers for more than 40 years, principally with the Hearst Corporation. For 16 years, he was general manager of the New York *Journal-American*. He served as publisher of the *San Francisco Examiner* from 1961-1975, when he joined the Hearst Foundation as vice president. He was twice nominated for the Pulitzer Prize. In the following viewpoint, Gould argues that the many legal protections offered to criminals have worked to the detriment of society.

As you read, consider the following questions:

1. To what does the author attribute higher crime rates?
2. According to Gould, how has the Miranda decision undermined the criminal justice system?
3. What proposals does the author make to improve the system?

Charles L. Gould, "The Evil Persons Who Brutalize Our Streets." Reprinted with permission from the Americanism Educational League.

Let's take a look at our own country today. Study the appalling moral erosions that are all too evident throughout the width and breadth of our fair land:
- —Educators speak out in favor of free love.
- —Publishers sell sex as a commercial commodity.
- —Movies and night clubs peddle pornography in productions of gutter filth.
- —TV pours out a flood of sick, brutal, and sadistic presentations.
- —Magazines and newspapers publish pictures and articles that violate the bounds of good taste.
- —Contraceptives and birth control counsel are endorsed for high school girls.

Look around you. These things are happening in our America. In the past two decades we have seen our national standards of morality lowered again and again. We have seen a steady erosion of past principles of decency and good taste. And—we have harvested a whirlwind. As our standards have lowered, our crime level and social problems have increased. Today we have a higher percentage of our youth in jail . . . in reformatories . . . on probation . . . and in trouble than ever before!

We have witnessed too the persuasive power of a small but articulate group of professional and non-professional apologists and psychiatric soothsayers who defend killers, rapists and thieves, and treat them as victims rather than as perpetrators of heinous crimes.

Bleeding Hearts

The warped logic of the men and women who are more concerned with bleeding hearts than with bleeding bodies goes something like this: "It is the system that is to blame. It is the ghetto. It is the lack of education. It is prejudice and poverty that forces young people to break the law."

In effect, they argue that you and I are guilty! It is easy to see how this faulty reasoning permits vicious criminals to rationalize and justify their violent acts. With this topsy-turvy kind of thinking, robbery, rape and murder become "moral acts against an immoral society."

Well, count me out! As I accept no credit for the great and good things done by tens of millions of men and women, neither do I accept blame for the actions of the evil persons with twisted minds who brutalize our streets. My sympathy and concern is, has been and will continue to be with those who are victimized rather than those who commit the crimes.

34

In my opinion, our problems with law-breakers have been ag-gravated by some of our courts. They have handed down deci-sions that seem to part company with past principles and tend to make a mockery out of justice. Rules and regulations that prevailed for generations as sane and sensible guidelines for per-sonal conduct were reduced, removed or ignored. As a result of decisions of activist courts, police officers are mandated to observe Marquis of Queensbury rules in dealing with punks and thugs.

In this climate of the new, and I believe, confused morality, we mollycoddle hardened criminals and release unreformed hoodlums to prey on society. I am unalterably opposed to legal loopholes which permit hardened, vicious criminals with long records of serious infractions to escape just and proper punish-ment. Unfortunately, the courts in a desire to protect the rights of the individual have too often ignored the rights of many. We too have rights!

Collapsing System

In 1981, there were 13 million serious crimes and only 2 million arrests (17 percent). But only about 160,000 felons actually went to jail—1 percent of serious crimes.

This means, 99 percent of all serious crimes were committed with impunity—a "success rate" that could never be matched by honest, diligent citizens engaged in any activity in the private sector.

Anyone who doesn't understand that felons know this is fatu-ously naive. The roving bands of young thugs are a testament to a massive breakdown in the criminal justice system.

Warren T. Brookes, *Conservative Digest*, May 1985.

As our laws and regulations have been eased and relaxed, we have found our crime rates soaring to new highs. According to a report by the F.B.I. that reached my desk recently:

—Every two seconds of every hour of every day throughout this year a major crime is committed in these United States.
—Every 23 minutes of every hour of every day, some innocent man, woman or child is murdered in our land.
—Every six minutes of every hour of every day, a woman is raped.

Crime Rate Up 400%

A few years ago, a wave of concern and indignation swept our nation when it was revealed that for the first time in our history, major crimes throughout the 50 states exceeded the 2 million mark. Last year more than 10 million major crimes were reported.

During these years, our nation's population increased about 15% while our crime rate soared 400%! Ironically, the skyrocketing crime rate closely parallels the increase in the cost of government. As tax-payers, we get taken at both extremes!

Let me cite a report that may cast some light on our frightening crime rate. A comprehensive nation-wide survey of persons arrested for major offenses during one four-year period in the 1970s showed the 65%—that's two out of three—had been arrested at least two times on earlier charges. Some had as many as 10 previous arrests. An earlier study of criminals paroled or dismissed showed that more than 85% were re-arrested in less than four years. In short, we are indulging in the costly and dangerous exercise of a revolving door approach to criminal justice.

Police Shackled

The highest court in the land—especially in the 1960s—handed down a series of decisions in criminal cases that gave more strength to individual rights than to the rights of society as a whole. There were decisions that protected the rights of the criminal to such a degree that they shackled our law enforcement officers in their responsibilities of protecting the public at large.

Judges are not appointed or elected to make laws. They are appointed or elected to *interpret* laws. The vast majority are committed to this philosophy. A few, however, shape decisions to reflect their personal views. After the labored struggle in the creation of our laws, it seems folly indeed to allow them to be warped or twisted to reflect the ideological colorations of some who administer them. But the record is clear. It does happen.

Take the infamous Escobedo decision which drastically altered some provisions of criminal law. Supreme Court Justice White, in his dissent which was concurred in by Justices Clark and Stewart, said, and I quote, "Law enforcement will be crippled and its task made a great deal more difficult for unsound, unstated reasons which can find no home in any of the provisions of the Constitution."

"Cocoon of Silence"

Take the equally infamous Miranda decision that wrapped each criminal in a protective cocoon of silence from the time of his capture until he met with his attorney. In the Miranda case, Supreme Court Justices Harlan, Steward and White joined Tom Clark in the dissent. They said, "The decision represents poor Constitutional law and entails harmful consequences for the country at large." They were right! These two decisions alone have resulted in the release of hundreds of self-confessed criminals throughout the 50 states and have placed a burden on police officers that boggles the mind.

Not only are voluntary confessions generally not admissible, but even a signed statement containing a paragraph stating that the confession is made voluntarily with full knowledge of legal rights is often considered an infringement of the criminal's rights and thus not acceptable. I submit that justice is frustrated and society is ill served when our courts employ trifling technicalities to release murderers, thieves and rapists.

To Reduce the Toll

Now, how can we cope with the cancerous evil of a crime wave that continues to increase across the width and breadth of our nation? How can we take steps to reduce the terrible toll from brutal beatings, muggings and killings?

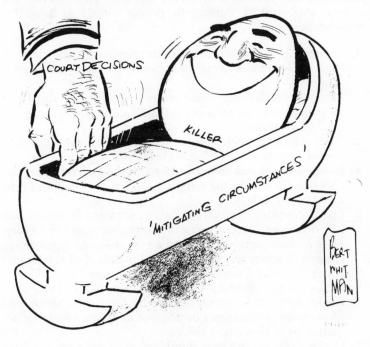

CODDLED EGG

A study of history reveals that the surest deterrent to crime is the absolute adherence of policies insuring swift and just punishment to all who break the law. This was the reasoning of our founding fathers when they wrote the Sixth Amendment to our Constitution guaranteeing speedy and public trials in all criminal prosecutions.

In recent years, however, the functioning of our courts has grown complex beyond belief. Attorneys have become expert in technical legal gymnastics that result in countless delays and countless appeals. Far too often, trials drag on for months or years. Witnesses die or disappear. Memories become fogged and weary. Evidence is lost or misplaced, and justice falls victim to its own safeguards.

Strangle Our System

I believe the time is overdue when bold steps should be taken to cut the tangle of legalistic red tape that threatens to strangle our judicial system. It would be presumptuous of me to attempt to spell out steps to improve our legal procedures while still preserving due process. However, I feel it is quite in order for me—as a concerned citizen—to propose goals at least for consideration:

1. I believe the legal process might be speeded if predetermined fines or sentences were established for more non-victim crimes.
2. I propose reclassifying some minor crimes and making them infractions or misdemeanors to permit elimination of long and costly jury trials.
3. Twelve is not a magic number for juries. I believe we should consider using 5, 6, or 7 members on a jury.
4. I propose local and state courts adopt the Federal system of choosing juries. Let the judges make the selection and thus avoid costly delays.
5. Let us consider eliminating the requirement of unanimous jury decisions. Presently, one dissenting vote can hang a jury. Does it make sense to demand a consensus among average citizens of a jury when the brilliant members of the United States Supreme Court may divide their vote five to four?
6. Let us accept voluntary confessions from criminal suspects. Confessions must not be elicited by force. Neither should spontaneous confessions be allowed to become tools for acquittal, as is now often the case.
7. I believe prison sentences should be mandatory for all crimes committed with guns.
8. I believe prison sentences should be mandatory for all persons convicted of selling hard dope.
9. I believe we should revise or remove the Exclusionary Rule. Today, for example, if a car is stopped for speeding and because of suspicious actions by the driver, the police conduct a search and find a pound of heroin, the evidence probably will not be acceptable in court. Why cannot such evidence be accepted under probable cause?
10. Plea bargaining has become the shadow court in our judicial

system. A man indicted for a crime can permit his attorney to plead him guilty to a lesser offense when assured a lesser penalty. We must not permit this device to be used as a means of releasing hardened criminals to continue preying on society.

Endless Appeals

I believe our best legal brains should be enlisted to establish workable rules and provisions to eliminate or curtail the endless appeals and postponements that presently slow the wheels of justice while causing monstrous legal fees. Public patience—and public pocketbooks—are at the breaking point. Steps must be taken to restore speedy trials while preserving justice!

4 $\overset{\text{VIEWPOINT}}{}$

---

*"The basic proposition of American criminal
justice is that every person is presumed
innocent until proven guilty."*

The Criminal Justice
System Must Protect
Accused Offenders

Bertram Harnett

Bertram Harnett is a widely-known judge. His many diverse accomplishments include stints as a trial judge, corporate lawyer,
Legal Aid Society president, politician, teacher, and author. In the
following viewpoint, Judge Harnett criticizes those people who
blame judges and the court system for allowing criminals to commit crimes without receiving adequate punishment. He argues that
the rights that protect the accused protect every citizen, and that
compromising these rights would end in harming the innocent.

As you read, consider the following questions:

1. What is the basic proposition of the criminal justice
   system, according to the author?
2. What part does Harnett say humanity plays in the criminal
   justice system?
3. What view does the author have of the media? Do you
   believe it is accurate?

From LAW, LAWYERS, AND LAYMEN, copyright © 1984 by Bertram Harnett. Reprinted
by permission of Harcourt Brace Jovanovich, Inc.

The basic proposition of American criminal justice is that every person is presumed innocent until proven guilty. A host of constitutional rights restrict the ways the state can go about proving guilt. United States Supreme Court cases, in past decades, have put procedural safeguards around such conduct as confessions, police search and seizure, right to speedy trial, police wiretaps, rights to counsel, self-incrimination, and identification. Trial judges are bound by high court rulings in the protection of constitutional rights, and in following them cannot be fairly taxed for malfeasance or softness. If changes in fundamental constitutional guarantees are thought desirable, either the United States Constitution must be amended or the United States Supreme Court persuaded.

Shortcuts across constitutional rights are dangerous ground, since the freedom of all of us is linked together. Those who would trade liberty for security must know that all the cliches about vigilance being the price of liberty are true, for what the government can do to one it can do to another. People become lulled where violent crimes are involved; after all, how many such criminally accused does the average person really know? It is only when civil rights deprivations strike home that most people become alert to their personal significance. Just as the national will to continue the Vietnam War crumbled as the military draft began to cut heavily into the middle classes, the criminal involvement of "nice" youngsters with drugs and "nice" adults with white-collar crimes has driven to unlikely homes the reminders of freedom's necessities.

Impatience with due process and other legal rights may also be ill-concealed manifestations of racism or ethnic hostility. There is an unfortunate tendency to aggregate guilt by class of person, particularly among racial and religious minorities, and the disadvantaged. The rights of these, and of the unpopular, are more apt to be forfeited when the panic is on.

Judges Take the Blame

Trial judges often take the blame for sloppy police work or poor preparation by the prosecution. If an acquittal results from a failure of evidence, the judge is likely to find himself blamed, particularly if provocative journalism has formed public opinion in the belief of guilt. The basic point, often overlooked, is that the accused person may simply not have been proven to be guilty. In plainer terms, the judge or jury found the accused "did not do it." The public, innocent of the actual facts of the trial, starts from

41

the immediate assumption that "he did do it." The public often assumes guilt based on the mere fact that a person was arrested. Even if the arrested party is never charged in court—as most felony arrestees are not—and even if he is discharged by the police or the prosecution without trial, the judges are still blamed by the public. Parole deficiencies that result in the premature release of prisoners (a function normally beyond the control of judges) and any violence these paroled prisoners may commit are often attributed to the trial judge. He is culpable for all the ills of the criminal-justice system; he takes the "rap" for the malfunctioning of society. A particularly ironic quirk is that judges are universally blamed for treating criminals too "softly," when it may have been the juries who actually mandated the protested verdicts.

Protecting the Accused Offsets Government's Power

Government's power to investigate, arrest, charge, try and punish its citizens is awesome. Power so overwhelming is subject to abuse. And abuse, whether deliberate or inadvertent, can deny justice to an individual accused of crime. That is why this country has attempted to build "massive safeguards" of defendants' rights into its criminal-justice system. Those safeguards, too, are subject to abuse, but the balance of power remains with the government.

Minneapolis Tribune, February 10, 1981.

"Judge" is a good active headline word. A story appeared in the *New York Times* (scarcely known to be a rabble-rousing newspaper) describing the judicial release of a teen-age gang member accused of involvement in a subway violence incident, which had earlier attracted considerable public notice:

A Guardian Angel Is Set Free by Judge

A Brooklyn judge has dismissed assault charges against a 17-year-old member of the Guardian Angels accused of fighting with two Transit police officers who had accused him of smoking in a subway station.

[Name deleted], a member of the volunteer group that fights subway crime, was cleared by Judge Alan I. Friess in Criminal Court *after a grand jury has declined on Wednesday to indict him on charges of assault and resisting arrest.* [Emphasis added.]

The charges stemmed from an altercation that took place Oct. 5 in the BMT Pacific Street station in Brooklyn.

While the headline plainly accuses the judge, it is mentioned only in passing that the dismissal of charges actually resulted from a grand jury's refusal to indict the suspect.

But are judges too lenient? Does judicial leniency result in so-called revolving-door justice, under which criminals are brought before a judge and then released to the streets without going to jail? The questions are critical, because there is obviously considerable activity around that revolving door in the nation's urban courthouses. Before the judiciary is condemned, critics should note any inconclusive police and prosecution work that fails to support the charges brought, the glut of the court calendar, the number of prison cells available, the lack of effective penal rehabilitation, and the relative seriousness of the crime charged against the numbers of more serious crimes imminently pending on the court docket faced by understaffed prosecuting officers with understaffed police support. Can the public accept that a shortage of typewriters in a district attorney's office may work a criminal processing bottleneck?

Some judges are doubtless too lenient as a result of sheltered existence and inexperience in criminal reality. Criminal law invokes tough decisions, with punishments to match, and there are judges who simply cannot stand this gaff. A mayor of New York City made an interesting observation in commenting on his city's crime difficulties. He questioned the value of merit selection of judges, and indicated he would go back to political recommendations for his appointees. He felt merit selection yielded scholars and theoreticians, but the political leaders would send street-smart judges more attuned to criminal realities. But my own observation is that, taken as a class, judges are harsher, much more inured to meting out punishment, than average citizens.

Public Distanced from Courtroom

Another force is at work; it is called humanity. The greatest calls for Draconian sentencing come from afar—from the society at large that seethes outside the courtroom. In the courtroom, judges and juries alike see the defendant as a person, not a photograph. The sympathetic emanations for mercy are strongest in the courtroom and fade out beyond. The most vivid analogy I can make of that contrast is the difference between an infantry soldier killing an enemy with a bayonet, close up, where he can smell his body and be drenched with the spray of his blood, and an Air Force bombardier dropping his bomb from tens of thousands of feet in the clear air, without challenge, on people who will forever be unknown and anonymous to him. The kill at the bar of justice is an infantry kill, infinitely harder than the one pressed by the bombardier at the bar of the local saloon.

Average citizens go to great lengths to avoid giving offense. Civilization operates on the assumption that other peoples' feelings must be accommodated. But judges and jurors must make and deliver in open court hard decisions over people they will come to know. Is it wholly unacceptable that they act with compassion when they see the defendant up close and become fully aware he is a person? Critics say that judges are paid to be objective, and if judges cannot stand the heat, they should get out of the courtroom. But judges are people. And the jurors, the conscience of the community, are not really paid at all, and they are conscripted into the courtroom.

Belief in the Courts

A necessary social factor in the scheme of criminal punishment is the belief that it works. On this rests the average person's confidence in the system, and his sense of security. The courts can and should do more than they do to inform the public of their activities. Cases of high public interest, particularly, must be explained in some meaningful manner. I was freshly reminded of this need when a Westchester County Court judge in New York State set aside, as contrary to the weight of the evidence, a jury verdict of guilty of arson against a young Hispanic man accused of setting a highly publicized hotel fire that resulted in the deaths of more than twenty people. Indeed, the newspapers had all but convicted the accused before the verdict. The public clamor against the judge was high, as might be expected, and no little bewilderment was evident. Why was a "guilty" man being set free? Why did the judge allow the issue to go to the jury if he was going to set aside a guilty verdict? The apparent answer is that the judge believed that if the appellate courts reversed him, no new jury would be required, since a jury had already spoken in the case, albeit unsatisfactorily to him. Right or wrong, the judge's action was courageous. In view of public interest and indignation, I felt the court system owed some explanation to its sponsors and supposed beneficiaries. Media accounts of trials are notoriously distortive, particularly through the trouble/action-oriented television camera, which tends to condense trials into a few unrepresentative seconds. Cases can never be judged from any media vantage point.

There is, at times, excessive preoccupation with the rights of the accused—often in neglect of the rights of the public and of the victim whose person or property has been violated. It is unquestionably in the public interest to arrest and punish criminals. The point must be made, obvious though it may seem, that criminal law is neither a game nor a contest. Judges must know the governing rules of fair prosecution, but they must also understand that the idea is not to throw out as many cases as possible on mechanical or farfetched applications of constitutional principle. They must shun legal gamesmanship and seek to understand the reason for the rules: to do justice for all. It is easier said than done.

"Adversary procedure has served as a guardian of individual liberty since its inception."

The Adversary System Guarantees Justice

Stephan Landsman

Stephan Landsman is a professor of law at the Cleveland-Marshall College of Law where he teaches torts, evidence, and legal process. In the following viewpoint, Landsman argues that the adversary system of justice, in which two parties oppose one another in a court of law, is uniquely suited to defending human rights. He believes that the control that each individual citizen maintains in his or her trial from beginning to end assures that individual rights remain paramount.

As you read, consider the following questions:

1. What are some of the common criticisms of the adversary system, according to Landsman? How does he refute these criticisms?
2. Why does the author defend the lawyer's role in the adversary system?
3. Does the author believe poor and underprivileged people have equal access to the courts? Why or why not?

Stephan Landsman, *The Adversary System: A Description and Defense.* Washington, DC: The American Enterprise Institute, 1984. Excerpts are reprinted with permission of American Enterprise Institute.

Critics have, in recent years, vigorously attacked the adversary system, claiming that it is flawed. These attacks have profoundly affected the debate concerning retention of adversary procedure and have greatly facilitated the adoption of nonadversarial methods. . . .

The . . . facets of the adversary system most strongly condemned as inhibitors of the discovery of truth are party control of the information-gathering process, zealous and single-minded representation of each litigant by his attorney, and evidentiary rules that circumscribe the types of information available to the decision maker. . . .

Zealous Representation of the Litigant

Attorneys have, from the earliest times, been viewed as obstructors of truth. The basis for this view is not hard to identify. Attorneys are skilled advocates. Their facility with words and procedure gives them the means of manipulating the information-gathering process. When the advocate lends his talents to the single-minded pursuit of the goals of his client, it is not hard to understand why onlookers might consider him the enemy of veracity. The ethical rule that compels the attorney zealously to represent his client officially reinforces loyalty at the expense of commitment to the search for truth.

In response it should first be noted that attorney zeal is directly linked to *party control of proceedings* and that the arguments in favor of party control also support zealous representation of the litigant. This is so because the complexity of legal proceedings makes it virtually impossible for parties to proceed without counsel. It has frequently been suggested that the attorney can serve his client and, at the same time, ensure that the truth is disclosed. This position fails to preserve attorney zeal and loyalty because it requires the attorney to act as an agent of the court whenever there is a potential conflict between his client's interests and the pursuit of material information. The likely results of casting the attorney in this impossible situation are unethical conduct if the lawyer chooses to act on behalf of his client in a doubtful case and substantial discouragement of client candor, cooperation, and trust if the lawyer chooses to act on behalf of the court.

This does not mean that an attorney can never be required to act in ways that oppose his client's wishes. When a client asks his lawyer to aid him in the commission of a crime or in a perpetration of a fraud, the attorney can and must reject such overtures. The situations in which the attorney must reject his client's wishes should be clearly and narrowly defined, however, otherwise a chill will be cast over the relationship and over the entire adversary process.

The rules of evidence prohibit a wide range of information from being presented to the fact finder. No matter how useful or important certain items may be, if they fall afoul of the evidence rules they cannot be considered. This applies to most words spoken out of court (hearsay) as well as to such facts as a party's criminal record or the existence of insurance. In all this the critics see a substantial barrier to the disclosure of important facts and, hence, an impediment to the discovery of truth.

Constitutional Guarantee

The most important constitutional recognition of adversary procedure is to be found in the Sixth and Seventh amendments to the Constitution. The Sixth Amendment requires that a jury be available in all criminal cases and that the accused have the right "to be confronted with the witnesses against him, to have compulsory process for obtaining witnesses in his favor, and to have the Assistance of Counsel for his defence." Taken together these requirements go a long way toward establishing adversary procedure in criminal cases.

Stephan Landsman, *The Adversary System*, 1984.

As in the case of attorney zeal, the rules of evidence serve, at least in part, to preserve party control of litigation. They achieve this result by curtailing judicial power over the admission and exclusion of evidence. The rules also directly protect the neutrality of the fact finder. While each rule may not be defensible on this ground, the general thrust of the rules is to insulate the decision maker from unreliable or prejudicial evidence. The protective function is of special importance when lay jurors decide cases. Protection also takes on added importance in the American adversary system because facts are presented only once, at the trial level. In these circumstances insulation from misleading material seems crucial because taint cannot be overcome by a *de novo* hearing on appeal.

Access to the Judicial System

Critics have advanced a number of other objections to the adversary system. They have argued that the American system fails to allow any but the wealthy and powerful access to counsel and the courts. The cost of litigation is said to be so great that the vast majority of Americans cannot afford to participate in the system. Substantial evidence indicates that cost does exclude some from participating in the justice system. Exclusion does not, however, result from any characteristic intrinsic to the adversary method but rather to the means by which it is presently implemented in the United States. Because the problem is not inherent in an adversarial system, it does not warrant the scrapping of the system. What is required is reform of the social and economic conditions that exclude a sizable segment of the population from access to the courts. . . .

The Power of the Attorney

A number of perceptive critics have argued that the attorneys upon whom the adversary system relies have become too dominant a force in the litigation they prosecute. The value of the adversary system is, in large part, attributable to party involvement in the litigation process. When the attorney comes to play too decisive a role, he can short-circuit the benefits of party control. In such circumstances the parties are likely to feel that they have not had a hand in the adjudication of the case and that they are not bound by the mandates of the court. Attorney domination can also cause an increase in "impositional costs" by focusing the litigation on the lawyer's interests rather than on the client's needs.

At present, it does not appear that the problem of attorney control is so grave as to threaten the integrity of the adversary system. Further, corrective mechanisms within the adversary framework help to ensure that the attorney will serve his client's interests. Perhaps most significant are the ethical rules governing attorney behavior. These compel the attorney to solicit and to obey his client's instructions with respect to settlement and crucial strategic decisions during the course of litigation. While it is uncertain whether attorneys will obey such rules, the heightened awareness of the lawyer's ethical responsibilities created by the Watergate scandal and reinforced by the American Bar Association's continuing activism in the ethics field provide a basis for optimism. In cases of serious deviation from a client's instructions, the injured litigant can seek damages in a malpractice action. The expanding scope of attorney malpractice liability has the beneficial effect of providing a means of enforcing the ethical rules regulating consultation and control. . . .

Benefits of Party Control of Litigation

A number of reasons . . . warrant reliance on adversarial methods. The adversary process provides litigants with the means to control their lawsuits. The parties are preeminent in choosing the forum, designating the proofs, and running the process. The courts, as a general rule, pursue the questions the parties propound. Ultimately, the whole procedure yields results tailored to the litigants' needs and in this way reinforces individual rights. As already noted, this sort of procedure also enhances the economic efficiency of adjudication by sharply reducing impositional costs.

Party control yields other benefits as well. Perhaps most important, it promotes litigant and societal acceptance of decisions rendered by the courts. Adversary theory holds that if a party is intimately involved in the adjudicatory process and feels that he has been given a fair opportunity to present his case, he is likely to accept the results whether favorable or not. Assuming this theory is correct, the adversary process will serve to reduce post-litigation friction and to increase compliance with judicial mandates.

Slow Pace Guarantees Justice

Almost every procedure in the adversary process moves at a measured pace rather than at maximum speed. Delay, or perhaps more accurately, deliberation, has been built into every aspect of the adversary system. If one adopts the view that any diminution in speed is a serious danger, then every part of the adversary process is open to challenge. The problem with this sort of challenge is that it fails to focus on the most important question, whether there is a need for a process that is careful, deliberative, and committed to airing the claims of each litigant fully rather than one that proceeds at maximum speed.

Stephan Landsman, *The Adversary System,* 1984.

Adversary theory identifies litigant control as important to satisfy not only the parties but society as well. When litigants direct the proceedings, there is little opportunity for the judge to pursue his own agenda or to act on his biases. Because the judge seldom takes the lead in conducting the proceedings, he is unlikely to appear to be partisan or to become embroiled in the contest. His detachment preserves the appearance of fairness as well as fairness itself. . . .

Role of the Judge

The adversary process assigns each participant a single function. The judge is to serve as neutral and passive arbiter. Counsel is to act as a zealous advocate. According to adversary theory, when each actor performs only a single function the dispute before the court will be resolved in the fairest and most efficient way. The strength of such a division of labor is that individual responsibilities are clear. The possibility that a participant in the system will face conflicting responsibilities is minimized. Each knows what is expected of him and can work conscientiously to achieve a specifically defined goal. When participants in the judicial process are confronted with conflicting obligations, it becomes difficult for them to discharge any of their duties satisfactorily. The more frequently they face conflict, the more likely it is that they will not perform their assigned part or will not perform it in a way that minimizes conflict rather than fully discharges their responsibilities. Among the greatest dangers in this regard are that the judge will abandon neutrality if encouraged to search for material truth and that the attorney will compromise his client's interests if compelled to serve as an officer of the court rather than as an advocate. In either case the probity of the process is seriously undermined. . . .

The proud history and constitutional status of the adversary system as well as the benefits to be derived from its individualizing effect are strong reasons for its retention. Adversary procedure has served as a guardian of individual liberty since its inception. It has facilitated the extension of personal rights to a wide range of minority groups. Given these facts and the absence of a clearly superior alternative, the American commitment to the adversary system ought to be maintained.

"Under the adversary system an exemplary lawyer is required to indulge in overkill to obtain as legal rights benefits that in fact may not be legal rights."

The Adversary System Allows Injustice

David Luban

David Luban is research associate at the Center for Philosophy and Public Policy at the Maryland Law School. In the following viewpoint, Luban criticizes lawyers for using the adversary system as an excuse for unethical behavior. Lawyers may bury evidence that appears harmful to their clients' cases, he argues, and behave in other ways that obstruct justice.

As you read, consider the following questions:

1. Why does the author say that no lawyer would agree that the best way to get at the truth is through the adversary system?
2. What two forces, constantly in conflict, affect lawyers' behavior, according to the author?
3. What is Luban's primary objection to the adversary system?

David Luban, "The Adversary System Excuse," from David Luban, ed., THE GOOD LAWYER: LAWYERS' ROLES AND LAWYERS' ETHICS (Totowa, NJ: Rowman & Allanheld, 1983), pp. 93-99, 117 & 118.

The question whether the adversary system is, all in all, the best way of uncovering the facts of a case at bar sounds like an empirical question. I happen to think that it is—an empirical question, moreover, [one] that has scarcely been investigated, and that is most likely impossible to answer. This last is because one does not, after a trial is over, find the parties coming forth to make a clean breast of it and enlighten the world as to what *really* happened. A trial is not a quiz show with the right answer waiting in a sealed envelope. We can't learn directly whether the facts are really as the trier determined them because we don't ever find out the facts. . . .

Given all this, it is unsurprising to discover that the arguments purporting to show the advantages of the adversary system as a fact-finder have mostly been nonempirical, a mix of a priori theories of inquiry and armchair psychology. . . .

Here is one. . . . If each side attempts to prove its case, with the other trying as energetically as possible to assault the steps of the proof, it is more likely that all the aspects of the situation will be presented to the fact-finder than if it attempts to investigate for itself with the help of the lawyers. . . .

Perhaps science proceeds by advancing conjectures and then trying to refute them, but it does not proceed by advancing conjectures that the scientist knows to be false and then using procedural rules to exclude probative evidence.

The two adversary attorneys, moreover, are each under an obligation to present the facts in the manner most consistent with the client's position—to prevent the introduction of unfavorable evidence, to undermine the credibility of opposing witnesses, to set unfavorable facts in a context in which their importance is minimized, to attempt to provoke inferences in their client's favor. The assumption is that two such accounts will cancel out, leaving the truth of the matter. But there is no earthly reason to think this is so; they may simply pile up the confusion. . . .

No Lawyer Believes the Premise

No trial lawyer seriously believes that the best way to get at the truth is through the clash of opposing points of view. If a lawyer did believe this, the logical way to prepare a case for trial would be to hire two investigators, one taking one side of every issue and one taking the other. After all, the lawyer needs the facts, and if those are best discovered through an adversary process, the lawyer would be irresponsible not to set one up. . . .

It is sometimes said, however, that the point of the adversary

" BREAK WHEN I TELL YOU....NO LOW PUNCHES....
NOW SHAKE HANDS AND COME OUT FIGHTING. "

system is *not* that it is the best way of getting at the truth, but rather the best way of defending individuals' legal rights. It is, in the words of the attorney general of Maryland, "a celebration of other values" than truth. Monroe Freedman points out that if the sole purpose of a trial were to get at the truth we would not have our Fourth, Fifth, and Sixth Amendment rights; that improperly obtained evidence cannot be used against us and that we cannot be required to testify against ourselves indicate that our society considers other values more central than truth. And, according to the theory we shall now consider, these other values have to do with legal rights. . . .

The argument we are considering . . . that, right to counsel aside, adversary advocacy is the best defense of our *other* legal rights.

The no-holds-barred zealous advocate tries to get everything the law can give (if that is the client's wish) and thereby does a better job of defending the client's legal rights than a less committed lawyer would do.

Put this way, however, it is clear that the argument trades on a confusion. My legal rights are *everything I am in fact legally entitled to*, not *everything the law can be made to give*. For obviously a good lawyer may be able to get me things to which I am not entitled, but this, to call a spade a spade, is an example of infringing my opponent's legal rights, not defending mine. Every lawyer knows tricks of the trade that can be used to do opponents out of their legal deserts—using delaying tactics, for example, to make it too costly for an opponent without much money to prosecute a lengthy suit even though the law is on his or her side.

To this it might be replied that looking at it this way leaves the opponent's lawyer out of the picture. Of course, the reply continues, no one is claiming that a zealous adversary advocate is attempting to *defend* legal rights: he or she is attempting to *win*. The claim is only that the clash of two such adversaries will in fact defend legal rights most effectively. . . .

Priding Themselves on Winning

It is obvious that litigators pride themselves on their won-lost record. The *National Law Journal* describes "the world's most successful criminal lawyer—229 murder acquittals without a loss!" and describes the Inner Circle, a lawyers' club whose membership requirement is winning a seven-figure verdict. You never know, of course—maybe each of these cases really had legal right on its side. And when a coin comes up heads 229 times in a row it may be fair, but there *is* another explanation. Lawyers themselves do not see the point of what they do as defending their clients' legal rights, but as using the law to get their clients what they want.

It is true, of course, that one way for society to guarantee that lawyers do their best to defend their clients' rights is to commit them to defending every claim a client has to a right, whether valid or not. That kind of overkill is reassuring to each client, of course. But suppose we look at it from the point of view of the whole process, rather than of the individual clients. It is hard to see then why an adversary system is the best defender of legal rights. Why not, for example, a system in which both attorneys are committed to defending the legal rights of both parties, if they seem to be getting trampled? I am not recommending such a system: my point is only that we have no reason at all to believe that when two overkillers slug it out the better case, rather than the better lawyer, wins.

Let me be clear about what the objection is. It is not that the flaw in the adversary system as a defender of legal rights is overkill on the part of the morally imperfect, victory-hungry lawyers. The objection is that under the adversary system an *exemplary* lawyer is required to indulge in overkill to obtain as legal rights benefits that in fact may not be legal rights. . . .

Lawyers Cannot Excuse Immoral Behavior

The adversary system possesses only the slightest moral force, and thus appealing to it can excuse only the slightest moral wrongs. Anything else that is morally wrong for a nonlawyer to do on behalf of another person is morally wrong for a lawyer to do as well. The lawyer's role carries no moral privileges and immunities.

This does not mean that zealous advocacy is immoral, not even when it frustrates the search for truth or violates legal rights. Sometimes frustrating the search for truth may be a morally worthy thing to do, and sometimes moral rights are ill served by legal rights. All I am insisting on is that the standards by which such judgments are made are the same for lawyers and nonlawyers. If a lawyer is permitted to puff, bluff, or threaten on certain occasions, this is not because of the adversary system and the Principle of Nonaccountability, but because in such circumstances, anyone would be permitted to do these things. Nothing justifies doing them on behalf of a predator.

Winning Not the Point

Law schools do not and cannot simply teach students law. They inescapably teach their students as well what kind of lawyer they should become, and what kind of person. And it seems that the kind of lawyer they should *not* become is one who wins any case at any cost. For when lawyers like that win, the rest of us lose.

Report from the Center for Philosophy and Public Policy, Winter 1984.

But, it will be objected, my argument leads to a paradox, for I have claimed to offer a vindication, albeit a weak one, of the adversary system, and therefore of the duties of partisan advocacy that it entails. Am I not saying that a lawyer may be professionally obligated to do A and morally obligated not to do A?

One Less Excuse

That is indeed what I am saying, but there is no contradiction here. The adversary system and the system of professional obligation it mandates are justified only in that, lacking a clearly superior alternative, they should not be replaced. This implies . . . that when professional and moral obligation conflict, moral obligation takes precedence. When they don't conflict, professional obligations rule the day. The Principle of Professionalism follows from the fact that we have an adversary system; the Principle of Non-accountability does not. The point of elaborating the former is to tell the lawyer what, in this system, professionalism requires—to say that it requires zeal, for example, even when cutting corners might be more profitable or pleasant. Professionalism can tell a lawyer not to cut corners; my point is that it cannot mandate him or her to cut throats. When moral obligation conflicts with professional obligation, the lawyer must become a civil disobedient.

Not that this is likely to happen. Lawyers get paid for their services, not for their consciences. But so does everyone else. As we do not expect the world to strike a truce in the war of all against all, we should not expect lawyers to. Shen Te, the Good Woman of Setzuan, says:

> I'd like to be good, but there's the rent to pay. And that's not all: I sell myself for a living. Even so I can't make ends meet, there's too much competition.

That, of course, is the way the world is, and criticizing an ideology won't change the world. The point of the exercise, I suppose, is merely to get our moral ideas straight: one less ideology is, after all, one less excuse.

"It is the 'ordinariness' of the jury that finally emerges as its unique strength."

The Jury System Works

Melvyn Bernard Zerman

In the controversy over the jury system, many people argue that it is in desperate need of reform. It is said that juries are required to handle complex cases that they simply cannot understand. In the following viewpoint, Melvyn Bernard Zerman takes issue with this common complaint: he believes that it is the very ordinariness of the jury that is important. Only twelve people taken randomly from different walks of life can truly judge another's crime. Zerman's interest in the workings of the American jury system was sparked by his own experience as a juror. He is the author of *Beyond a Reasonable Doubt: Inside the American Jury System* from which this viewpoint is excerpted.

As you read, consider the following questions:

1. Why does Zerman argue that judges and lawyers should not replace juries?
2. The author grants that the jury system is imperfect, and yet believes it must be left in place. Why?
3. Does the author believe the jury serves its function well? Why or why not?

Attacked and belittled, the jury system, with all its flaws, survives. How come? Simply because, like democracy in Winston Churchill's famous remark, it remains "the worst form . . . except for all those other forms that have been tried from time to time."

As we begin our defense of the jury system, let us consider what its severest critics would offer in its place: a single judge or a panel of legal experts—that is, X number of people well-trained in the law, presumably attorneys and/or judges. These alternatives to the laymen jury would, of course, enjoy the services of persons who are highly intelligent and eminently capable of keeping their attention fixed on the trial at hand and their prejudices tightly controlled. Like the judges and, increasingly, the panels of lawyers that hear and render verdicts in the great majority of civil suits, the criminal trial experts would be expected to have no trouble following the most complicated testimony, and, more important, they would recognize dishonesty in witnesses and deviousness in attorneys far better than jurors generally can.

What we have just described is an ideal. Let us now look at the reality: just how well are lawyers and judges likely to perform in determining guilt or innocence? To answer that question, let's look at how well they perform their present duties.

It is not our purpose to investigate or expose or even evaluate the legal profession, but having subjected jurors to all manner of stinging comment, it is only fair to note that none other than the Chief Justice of the United States has repeatedly commented on the "ineptness, the bungling, the malpractice which can be observed in courthouses all over the country." The rich and, much more frequently, the poor complain about the quality of the legal services available to them. There are, of course, thousands of thoroughly qualified attorneys—capable, hardworking, ethical men and women—in practice today. But there are thousands of others who—whether they be rated by seasoned courtroom spectators, judges, jurors, law school professors, or their own clients— would get considerably less than passing grades.

Judges Criticized

As for the judges, they, too, have . . . been the target of heavy criticism. Not so long ago a national magazine featured on its cover the small head of a judge timidly emerging from a mountainous judicial robe, one many sizes too large for the perplexed-looking man inside it. The illustration embodied the message: many judges cannot fill the job they have been entrusted to do. Whether appointed or elected, judges are all too frequently seen as political hacks who have attained their seats on the bench not by their knowledge or accomplishments but by staying in the good graces of political party chieftains. In some of the more common complaints, judges are accused of being arrogant, corrupt, lazy, incompetent to the point of senility, and—an old friend—bigoted. (We should note, for example, that in the little chamber of the jury-trial horrors we just visited, all the guilty verdicts were upheld on appeal by judges who chose not to recognize the bias on which those verdicts were based.)

Again, the obvious truth is that there are superb judges serving in courtrooms everywhere—people not only of great legal experience but also of wisdom, understanding, compassion, discipline, patience, fairness, and total integrity. Whether rare or common in a government of laws not men, it is these exemplary guardians of justice who make the laws work.

Juries Support Democracy

The concept of the jury system is as close as any society has ever come to true democracy. Yet in today's complicated and precarious world, where competent social decisions require more, not less, citizen involvement, the jury system seems a burden. It draws criticism that is often unrelated to its actual performance and blame for poorly executed justice.

However, a scratch of the surface of so-called bad decisions will often expose underlying factors for which no jury can be blamed. This is not to say that the jury system functions without flaw, or that there aren't ways to help it function better. But in an age when it is increasingly difficult for individuals to feel they can have an impact on events, the jury remains a refuge where each individual's reasoning affects a collective result. . . .

The fact that the jury system tends to be idiosyncratic—even rambunctious—makes it a convenient target. Yet, its unpredictability is its inherent strength. The jury system brings a pot-au-feu approach to justice, and for all its potential chaos, it works at least as well as a great thick soup does when one is hungry.

Paula DiPerna, *Juries on Trial*, 1984.

But, in the eyes of many of us, apparently, the laws do not work well enough. In a 1978 poll of the population in general and of judges, lawyers, and community leaders in particular, public confidence in state and local courts ranked below that of the medical profession, police, business, and public schools. Can anyone question that it is the judges and the lawyers who must bear the major responsibility for this absence of trust?

If, then, lawyers and judges are, on the whole, performing their present roles rather less than impressively, surely it is misguided to thrust upon them the additional function of the laymen jury. But the case against the suggested alternatives to the jury system goes considerably deeper than that. For the sake of argument, let's assume that only the most dedicated and able men and women of the law, of the highest judicial caliber, were called on to replace juries in our criminal trials. What happens then is not something we can only imagine, for the fact is that all fifty states permit a defendant, except in the most extraordinary circumstances, to waive his right to a jury trial and appear before a judge alone, a procedure known as a *bench trial.*At least a third of the men and women tried for major crimes do put their trust in the judge. But statisical analysis shows that the more serious the crime charged, the more likely the accused is to opt for a jury trial. One study shows jury waivers in 70 percent of drug violation cases, 50 percent of forgery cases, 32 percent of robbery cases, and only 13 percent of murder cases. That same study indicates that defendants or, more realistically, their lawyers, have good reason for choosing as they do: the more serious the crime, the more likely a jury is to acquit.

Other studies have shown quite consistently that in jury trials the judge agrees with the jury's verdict about 75 percent of the time. In a tiny percentage of the cases, judges are inclined to acquit while the jury convicts. *But in about 20 percent of the cases, juries are more lenient than judges would have been.* Either they acquitted when the judge would have convicted, or they convicted on a lesser charge than the judges would have. In that finding, the difference between the jury system and its suggested alternatives stands revealed. . . .

Differences in Opinion

Where these differences in thinking between judge and jury exist—and, remember, they exist to a significant extent in no more than one case in five—they are not the product of chance or accident. The judge is a figure of authority, trained in the law, experienced in dealing with crime and criminals. It is to be *expected* that he will see people, events, and laws differently from ordinary citizens. Indeed it was in reaction to this very fact that the jury system came into being. As a symbol of democracy, it was intended to bring the perspectives of ordinary citizens to questions of justice. If our government is, as Lincoln said, "of the people, by the people, and for the people," the people should be able to decide if one of their number has violated a law of the state. The judge alone is too good for this task and therefore not good enough. Because he is of high social and economic standing, he may not accurately reflect the prevailing values of the community. Because he has been so often exposed to lawbreakers, he may let his knowledge of the past cloud his perception of the present. Because he is deeply schooled in the law, he may consider it more precious than freedom is to the rest of us. Because he is a figure of authority, he may not identify with the ordinary man who stands before him.

Thus, it is the "ordinariness" of the jury that finally emerges as its unique strength. What sets the jury system apart from all other methods of determining guilt or innocence is that ideally it alone allows a person to be judged by others just like him—people who come from the same community and share its values, people who have had similar experiences, people who have been tempted and have not always resisted, people who feel remorse for what they have done and perhaps regret for what they have not done, people who know how thin the line between guilt and innocence sometimes is. If juries are more inclined to be lenient than judges, it is because in any randomly selected group of twelve or even six, there may be a few men and women who will think and say much sooner than any judge could:

"From the time he was born that guy's life has been one bad break after another."

"My husband deserted me and I had to raise two kids all by myself. I know what it's like when you can't give them a Christmas present."

"Okay, so they broke into the building and burned the records. What were the records for, anyway? To send eighteen-year-olds over to die in a country no one ever heard of.". . .

Jurors Remain Interested

Juries make errors, but there has never been proof that the errors they make are "excessive," at least in relation to the unique components they provide: community values and impartiality. Because each case is a fresh matter for the jury, jurors are a lot closer to what Samuel Coleridge wrote is required of the reader of poetry: "a willing suspension of disbelief." The juror, much more than the judge, views each witness as sincere, each lawyer as dedicated, each oath as potentially inviolable. Judges are processors and can be, to put it mildly, jaded by the case traffic in which they are snarled each day. The jury, on the other hand, gives its best attention to each case, usually as free of preconceptions as possible and unpolluted by previous cases.

Paula DiPerna, *Juries on Trial,* 1984.

"I've lived long enough to know that nothing ever happens without a reason and sometimes—not always, but sometimes—the reason makes all the difference. A man who steals to eat shouldn't be treated like a man who steals to buy himself a Mercedes. I'm not saying the first man shouldn't be punished, but more often than not, it seems to me he gets punished a lot worse than the second man. And it should be just the opposite."

Jurors who make comments like these probably know little about law books and legal precedents. But without instruction they are doing exactly what the law wants them to do. Juries, in reaching their verdicts—verdicts they are commanded to pronounce but never to justify—are expected to draw upon their own humanity, upon what they have learned by living. If this makes them more compassionate, more willing to forgive, more accepting of error, and more inclined to doubt than a judge—whose every decision requires explanation—would be, the benefit to the defendant is precisely what our legal system would have him enjoy. For even with the presumption of innocence, a defendant is no more than one person against the state, and the odds he faces are great. Juries bring those odds just a bit more into balance.

Imperfect, but Working

The jury system in America today is sadly imperfect. It is in need of all kinds of reform and improvement. Yet most of the time it works. Although a noted turn-of-the-century philosopher described a jury as "twelve people of average ignorance," survey after survey has shown that however their minds may wander, most jurors remember what must be remembered; however unsophisticated their backgrounds, most jurors understand fully the case at hand—the evidence, the indictment, the law. . . .

For jurors in criminal cases are usually better than the rest of us; paradoxically, they are better than themselves. When they step into a jury box, they feel challenged as they have probably never been before. They know so much depends on them that they try as hard as they can to apply their intelligence and their common sense and their learning to the task at hand. They never forget who or what they value, but at the same time they recognize that other people may be the same or different without being any less deserving of justice.

We are being too idealistic, no doubt. Not all jurors rise to such heights. Some remain mired in their prejudices and therefore blind to the facts. But enough do not to allow a system that begins with ordinary people, chooses among them in the most haphazard and frequently unfair way, and treats the chosen with minimal courtesy and concern—to allow such a system to achieve compassionate justice with impressive regularity. It is exhilarating to be part of such a system. True, jury duty can often be a burdensome ordeal, but just as often it can be a stimulating challenge, a chance to take part in a real-life drama, and an occasion to learn about other people—and yourself. A summons to serve may sometimes prove to be a ticket to two weeks of boredom, but just as often it can be passport into a world you will enter as a stranger and leave as an honored citizen.

VIEWPOINT

"If we do not soon modernize the jury system and correct its obvious flaws, the most serious result will be a continued erosion of respect for the rule of law."

The Jury System Must Be Reformed

Norman A. Adler

Norman A. Adler is a member of the New York bar. He served as a special assistant to the US attorney general from 1938-1945. In the following viewpoint, Adler argues that juries are asked to give rulings on cases that are far too complex for lay people to decide. He believes that lawyers and judges should be more involved in deciding these cases—and in some cases, alternatives to a jury trial should be used.

As you read, consider the following questions:

1. What examples does the author give to prove that juries are incompetent to decide complex cases?
2. What alternatives to juries does the author suggest?
3. Do you agree with Adler's suggestions? Why or why not?

Norman A. Adler, "Complex Cases Call for 'Blue Ribbon' Juries," *The Wall Street Journal*, October 4, 1985. Reprinted with the author's permission.

If one of these days you notice that the statue of "Justice" has removed her blindfold, don't be surprised: She is probably taking a hard look at the breakdown of the jury system.

As society becomes more complex, more and more trials involve highly technical questions. Juries are being called upon to make factual findings about intricate subjects with which most of their members are not even remotely familiar.

Consider medical malpractice. These lawsuits usually rest on a determination of whether correct diagnostic or therapeutic procedures were followed. In many of these cases, not even the sky is the limit to money damages claimed and awarded. In 1983, awards nationwide were more than $2 billion and rising.

According to a study by the American Medical Association, the average settlement, less than $5,000 in 1979, has increased to more than $330,000. But the average is peanuts compared with the more spectacular examples. A baby girl in Brooklyn, N.Y., was awarded more than $29 million for disabilities resulting from an incorrect diagnosis of meningitis. In a California case involving respiratory failure, the plaintiff won so liberal a settlement that if he lives until the age of 75 he would receive an incredible $120 million.

Only Medical Doctors Could Reach Verdict

Other cases turning on medical considerations are just as hard for juries to deal with. In the second Claus von Bulow trial, the jury found the defendant not guilty of attempting to murder his wife by injecting her with insulin. It was able to reach this verdict only after running a gauntlet of conflicting conclusions and opinions from a veritable board of medical examiners—most of whom were summoned by counsel for the defendant.

Without benefit of a medical-school degree—any medical doctor would probably be excluded lest he or she unduly influence the deliberations—the von Bulow jurors had to thread their way through endocrinology, hematology, pathology, neurology, pharmacology, toxicology, and general and internal medicine—to list just some of the disciplines exhaustively explored.

Juries Cannot Understand

At the conclusion of their courtroom crash course, the jurors were turned loose in a mine field of forensic medicine. It would be remarkable indeed if that or any other ordinary jury could have cut through the welter of conflicting expert opinions to arrive at correct conclusions. Was justice served or subverted by imposing such a heavy burden on these non-expert jurors? How would a defendant of more modest means than Mr. von Bulow, assisted by outstanding doctors and criminal lawyers, have fared with the same jury?

Libel cases pose a challenge to juries because of the legal subtleties involved. The need to identify "truth" and "malice" in such cases is confusing enough to provide material for endless disputations in the law journals. Nevertheless, juries can be quite generous with a losing defendant's money. In these cases, however, the large awards are usually drastically reduced by the trial judge or appellate courts.

Antitrust lawsuits for damages require jurors to become instant experts in trade regulation. Were sales made at or below cost and were the costs accurately computed? Does a monopoly exist or

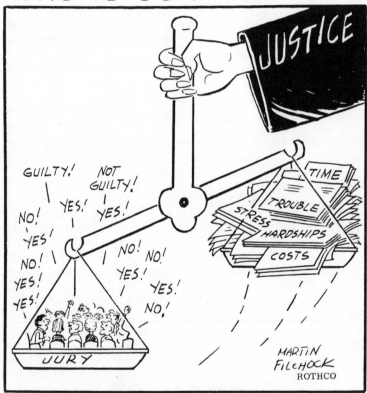

© Filchock/Rothco

are there interchangeable products?

The arcane nature of these questions inevitably leads to excessive and, in some cases, astronomically high jury awards. The MCI Communications Corp. suit against American Telephone & Telegraph Co. is a notorious example. A jury found that AT&T had unlawfully restricted access to the long-distance telephone market, and awarded MCI damages that, when trebled as provided by statute, amounted to $1.8 billion. Not surprisingly, this award was set aside on appeal. On a retrial, MCI received only 6% of the original award.

Assisting the Jury

Clearly, our legal procedures need improvement. A jury may be neither necessary nor desirable in all civil cases. In cases involving complex technical matters, judges should urge the parties to submit to arbitration or mediation. If a jury is nevertheless requested—most likely by a plaintiff hoping for a big award—its members should be chosen from a select "blue ribbon" panel. The judge should be free to assist it by commenting on the weight and reliability of the evidence.

In appropriate instances, independent impartial experts of acknowledged competence could be called upon to assist the jury in reaching a correct verdict and calculating a reasonable award to an injured party. These procedures alone would be likely to deter some litigants from risking an uncertain result in a costly jury trial. A more far-reaching proposal should also be considered—allow such experts to be the sole arbiters of technical aspects of complex cases.

More Power to the Judge

Trials should be speeded up. Those plodding on for weeks, even months, are an intolerable burden for jurors with full-time jobs. Too much time is now taken for jury selection. In English courts the jury box is filled quickly. We should adopt the practice of having only the judge conduct the voir dire—the preliminary examination of prospective jurors.

Many trials could be shortened if judges more strictly limited the introduction of evidence—rigorously excluding the cumulative, peripheral or repetitive. The use of independent experts would, no doubt, speed the proceedings.

A number of jurisdictions have already shrunk the size of juries and other jurisdictions are moving in that direction. In criminal courts only six jurors sit in misdemeanor trials. In civil cases only five of the six jurors need reach agreement on a verdict. The effects are salutary: Fewer citizens are inconvenienced by jury duty, trials move along more quickly, verdicts are easier to arrive at, and the incidence of hung juries is lessened.

These and similar proposals for changing the jury system require that a fine line be drawn between achieving greater efficiency and protecting the impartial administration of justice. The integrity of the jury system must be preserved as a constitutional bulwark against judicial or bureaucratic abuse and excess. It will not be easy to decide which changes are most desirable and will work best. The task will require the attention of our best legal minds. If we do not soon modernize the system and correct its obvious flaws, the most serious result will be a continued erosion of respect for the rule of law.

a critical thinking activity

Recognizing Deceptive Arguments

People who feel strongly about an issue use many techniques to persuade others to agree with them. Some of these techniques appeal to the intellect, some to the emotions. Many of them distract the reader or listener from the real issues.

Bob Dix, *Union Leader*. Reprinted with permission.

The cartoon above illustrates one extreme example of a deceptive argument. The cartoonist uses a strawperson technique: He distorts an opponent's ideas to make his own seem stronger. While many liberals believe that the reasons some people commit crime involve their upbringing or economic status, few would blame a bloodthirsty murderer's acts on the public at large. The cartoonist, then, is exaggerating his opponent's—in this case, liberals—arguments to bolster his own.

Below are listed a few common examples of argumentation tactics. Most of them can be used either to advance an argument in an honest, reasonable way or to deceive or distract from the real issues. It is important for a critical reader to recognize these tactics in order to rationally evaluate an author's ideas.

    a. *bandwagon*—the idea that "everybody" does this or believes this

    b. *scare tactics*—the threat that if you don't do or believe this, something terrible will happen

    c. *strawperson*—distorting or exaggerating an opponent's ideas to make one's own seem stronger

    d. *personal attack*—criticizing an opponent *personally* instead of rationally debating his or her ideas

    e. *testimonial*—quoting or paraphrasing an authority or celebrity to support one's own viewpoint

    f. *deductive reasoning*—the idea that since a and b are true, c is also true

    g. *slanters*—to persuade through inflammatory and exag·gerated language instead of reason

    h. *generalizations*—using statistics or facts to generalize about a population, place, or thing

The following activity will allow you to sharpen your skills in recognizing deceptive reasoning. Most of the statements below are taken from the viewpoints in this chapter. *Beside each one, mark the letter of the type of deceptive appeal being used. More than one type of tactic may be applicable. If you believe the statement is not any of the listed appeals, write N.*

1. The criminal justice system has many victims, and most of them are innocent.

2. So many of those in our prisons are poor that I doubt they would have committed the crimes that got them in prison if they had not suffered the disabilities of poverty.

3. Everyone agrees that poverty is no excuse for hurting other people.

4. Some people are lured into crime because it is highly profitable. Therefore, just giving criminals legitimate jobs will not work if the jobs are less profitable than crime.

5. Appalling moral erosions are all too evident throughout the width and breadth of our fair land, as evidenced by television, which pours out a flood of sick, brutal, and sadistic presentations.

6. Just as the criminal law limits the ways in which homosexuals express their sexual desires, so it limits the ways in which the poor can alleviate the miseries of poverty.

7. The warped logic of the men and women who are more concerned with bleeding hearts than bleeding bodies goes something like this: "It is prejudice and poverty that forces young people to break the law."

8. It is quite obvious that the courts care more about the rights of criminals than the rights of victims. As Justices Harlan, Stewart, and White said in their dissent to the *Miranda* decision, "The decision entails harmful consequences for the country at large."

9. We must curtail the endless and useless appeals being made by the criminals in this country—these actions are hitting every pocketbook of every taxpayer.

10. The principles that guide the adversary system are hogwash. No trial lawyer seriously believes that the best way to get at the truth is through the clash of opposing views.

11. It is obvious that lawyers pride themselves on their won-lost record. *The National Law Journal* describes "the world's most successful criminal lawyer—229 murder acquittals without a loss!"

12. Those that argue that a unanimous jury is the only way to achieve justice are idiots who care little about saving the taxpayers' money.

13. It is only logical that victims should want to exact punishment upon the criminals who victimized them.

14. Crime in the United States is up by 300 percent—which goes to show that the criminal justice system is incapable of dealing with crime.

Periodical Bibliography

The following list of periodical articles deals with the subject matter of this chapter.

Donald C. Becker — "The Expanding Criminal Justice System: Implications for the Future," *USA Today*, January 1982.

Vincent Bentivenga — "Is 11 Enough?" *American Bar Association Journal*, August 1985.

Kenneth B. Clark — "In Cities, Who Is the Real Mugger?" *The New York Times*, January 14, 1985.

Christie Davies — "Some Causes of Crime," *Current*, March/April 1983.

T.A. Demetrio — "Should Juries Decide Complex Cases?" *Trial*, August 1985.

Lilian S. Fisher — "The Rules of Evidence," *Newsweek*, September 29, 1986.

M.A. Kotler — "Reappraising the Jury's Role as Finder of Fact," *Georgia Law Review*, Fall 1985.

P.R. Lees-Haley — "Psychology of Jury Selection," *Res Gestae*, June 1985.

Richard Moran — "More Crime and Less Punishment," *Newsweek*, May 7, 1984.

Jane Bryant Quinn — "Justice for the Poor?" *Newsweek*, April 12, 1982.

John Rees — "An Interview with U.S. District Judge Herbert S. Stern," *The Review of the News*, April 25, 1984.

S.A. Saltzburg — "Lawyers, Clients, and the Adversary System," *Mercer Law Review*, Winter 1986.

David U. Strawn and G. Thomas Munsterman — "Helping Juries Handle Complex Cases," *Judicature*, March/April 1982.

William Tucker — "Bring Back the Jury," *The American Spectator*, August 1986.

D.E. Vinson — "How To Persuade Jurors," *American Bar Association Journal*, October 1985.

John R. Wennersten — "The Jury Is Out," *Inquiry*, December 1983.

Is the Litigation Crisis Destroying the Legal System?

CRIMINAL JUSTICE

"The fact that Americans are extremely litigious cannot be disputed."

America Is a Litigious Society

Charles H. Whitebread and John Heilman

Charles H. Whitebread is the George T. Pfleger Professor of Law at the University of Southern California and John Heilman is an attorney in Los Angeles. In the following viewpoint, Whitebread and Heilman argue that it is the attitude of the American public that has caused the liability crisis the country is experiencing. They believe it is a unique combination of social, political, and legal qualities that simply make Americans one of the most litigious peoples in the world.

As you read, consider the following questions:

1. How does America's "melting pot" society affect its litigiousness, according to the authors?
2. How do the authors relate the lack of cohesive neighborhoods to litigiousness?
3. How, according to Whitebread and Heilman, does America's commitment to equality generate pressure on the court system?

Charles H. Whitebread and John Heilman, "Why Are We So Litigious?" *Los Angeles Times*, December 21, 1983. Reprinted with permission.

California Chief Justice Rose Elizabeth Bird . . . proposed that sufficient tax revenues be generated to pay the full cost of trial courts. Her idea was designed to eliminate filing and user fees and to ensure equal access to civil courts for all Californians, especially the middle class. It drew strong criticism from some lawyers and laymen who felt that litigants, not taxpayers, should bear the costs of civil courts.

Regardless of the merits of the proposal, the debate may serve only to cloud the real issue: Why are so many people involved in legal disputes? Until that question is answered, the issue of who should pay for our dispute-resolution system is premature. Indeed, before any meaningful reform of our civil courts, we must address the issue of why our society is so litigious.

Americans Are Litigious

The fact that Americans are extremely litigious cannot be disputed. In the last 10 years we have heard constant complaints about crowded court calendars and burgeoning dockets. On the federal level there have even been proposals to create an intermediate appellate court between the Court of Appeals and the Supreme Court.

In state and local systems numerous proposals have been made and enacted to relieve congestion in the courts. Among these have been mandatory arbitration and the use of neighborhood dispute-resolution centers. But while some of these programs are quite successful, they have not had much effect on our litigiousness. The system is still overcrowded—and, as Bird has pointed out, there are people who want to use the courts but are deterred by high filing and user fees.

Why are Americans so litigious? One obvious explanation is that the structure and nature of our society are different. We are truly a melting pot of economic classes, and the juxtaposition of different cultures and values can often result in conflict. In addition, our traditions of independence and rugged individualism often mean that Americans are more likely to challenge the social order to correct a perceived wrong. When this is combined with our supposed materialism, a great deal of litigation may ensue.

Another potential explanation lies in the breakdown of other, less formal, methods of resolving disputes. In many societies strong extended families probably resolve many disputes and prevent others from occurring. But in the United States, with a high divorce rate and few extended families, the institution of the family rarely serves to resolve or avoid disputes, and in many cases may actually cause or exacerbate the sort of conflict that leads to

74

litigation.

Neighborhood pressure often resolves disputes, but in the United States our neighborhoods (such as they are) may actually increase litigiousness by bringing together people who have little in common. The transient nature of our society aggravates the problem because people feel less compunction about resorting to the legal system; after all, one or all of the disputants may leave the community. Obviously, people who have lived and worked in the same neighborhood for many years have a greater incentive to keep the peace by resolving their disputes outside the courts.

In our legal system lawyers are permitted to take cases on a contingent-fee basis. (Cases may be filed in which attorneys' fees are paid out of any potential recovery.) Generally this means that an attorney will take a case with an agreement to accept one-third of any recovery as a legal fee. Obviously the contingent fee lets some people pursue litigation that they otherwise could not afford.

American Notion of Equality

At the same time, our strong commitment to equality generates pressure on the legal system to guarantee equality of access to our courts. Everyone must have his day in court. Certainly our notion of equality, foreign to so many societies, contributes to the high volume of lawsuits in our courts. And we don't assess costs

Reprinted with permission of Heritage Features Syndicate.

against the losing parties. Elsewhere, notably in England, losing parties must pay the costs of litigation. This discourages some people from bringing frivolous lawsuits, and encourages others to settle quarrels without resort to the legal system. (By contrast, we sometimes award attorneys' fees to victorious litigants. Fees are even awarded at times to encourage certain types of litigation that are deemed socially advantageous.)

Impossible To Right All Wrongs

So what are we trying to accomplish with our legal system? Like no other society, we have attempted to use it to right all the wrongs and to remedy all the injustices of our society. And we use it not only more frequently but also for a greater variety of issues. We use law to eradicate inequality, and we use law to regulate a host of social, economic and even medical problems that are customarily resolved in non-legal ways in other countries.

Perhaps this litigiousness signifies the disintegration of our social fabric into competing materialistic factions. Or perhaps it is a sign of strength. Maybe the frequent resort to the legal system is the only way in which our diverse social factions can coexist in a peaceful and civilized manner.

Maybe—but maybe our legal system is overburdened because we ask it to do too much. Now may be the time to question whether the law can ever do all that we want it to do.

"Litigation actually occurs in a very tiny percentage of all disputes."

America Is Not Overly Litigious

John W. Cooley

John W. Cooley, a former federal magistrate, is in private law practice in Chicago and serves as an arbitrator, mediator, and consultant in alternative dispute resolution. He co-teaches a course on alternatives to litigation at Loyola University of Chicago School of Law. In the following viewpoint, Cooley argues that statistics prove the United States does not have a higher rate of litigation than other industrialized societies. He concludes that Americans' litigiousness is simply a myth.

As you read, consider the following questions:

1. The author states that people commonly believe that lawyers create litigation because they want higher fees. How does he refute this?
2. What facts does Cooley cite to prove America is not a litigious society?
3. What kinds of alternatives are already being practiced, according to the author? How does this refute another commonly held notion?

John W. Cooley, "Puncturing Three Myths About Litigation," *ABA Journal*, December 1984. Reprinted with permission from the *ABA Journal*, The Lawyer's Magazine.

Winston Churchill once said: "I always avoid prophesying beforehand; it is a much better policy to prophesy after the event has already taken place." But unfortunately that's not possible when predicting the future of alternatives to litigation in the federal court—the future of what I call "unlitigation."

Three key elements of federal court "unlitigation" are: (1) the court system, (2) the types of alternatives in use and (3) lawyers. With respect to each of these elements there is at least one myth held generally by the public. I hope to dispel these myths and clear the way for credible prophecies.

The Explosion Myth

One myth about the court system currently pervades the literature and appears to be accepted unquestioningly by society in general. The myth is that America is experiencing a "litigation explosion" in its trial courts that forecasts certain doom of its legal systems.

This explosion theme was introduced in the early 1970s, but it is based on speculation and unsupported pronouncement. "Per capita rates of litigation in the United States—public opinion notwithstanding—are not the highest in the world. About all you can say is that we are higher than the average," said former ABA President Wallace Riley at the ABA annual meeting last August. "The incidence of lawsuits in this country is in the same general range as those of England, Australia, New Zealand and Ontario, Canada—which share our general level of economic development, as well as a common legal tradition."

Marc Galanter of the University of Wisconsin Law School, of-fers some intriguing statistics derived from court studies and historical data. For example:

• Approximately 88 percent of all civil cases filed in American courts are settled.

• More than 30 percent of those cases are not even formally con-tested. They are withdrawn, abandoned or defaulted.

• Federal courts handle only a tiny fraction of all the cases filed in the United States. In 1975, for example, 7.27 million cases—civil, criminal and juvenile—were filed nationwide; only 160,000 of them were filed in federal courts. . . .

This discussion reduces to one issue: whether the federal trial court "litigation explosion" is a myth. If society is at worst only slightly more litigious than it ever was, what is causing the percep-tion of massive system overload, of litigation cataclysm, of judicial doomsday? The answer lies not in quantity but rather in the quality or nature of the federal trial court's caseload. . . .

78

There has been a burgeoning of pretrial and post-trial activities to the point that the trial is no longer the center of gravity of the litigated case. More massive and elaborate formal law has spawned "lawsuits before lawsuits." Large and complex cases involve a huge investment of judicial time. A growing portion of judicial time is directed away from civil disputes to criminal cases because of the Speedy Trial Act. All this together has caused the bench and bar to seek out alternatives to conventional processing of disputes by federal district courts. What are these alternatives?

The commonly perceived notion of the public and the legal profession about alternative dispute resolution is that it is a relatively new concept, having its origin in the early 1970s. It is time that this myth is put to rest. The truth of the matter is that "unlitigation" has been utilized in America by businesses and courts for more that 100 years. . . .

Facts Do Not Support the Rhetoric

That our courts are suffering the effects of a "litigation explosion" and facing an immediate crisis is considered axiomatic in both professional and lay circles. Court business, the argument goes, has changed drastically in both its nature and quantity. Concomitantly, Americans are portrayed as being excessively, almost pathologically litigious, willing to "sue the bastards" with the slightest provocation and over the most trivial matters. There is, however, a growing skepticism about the alleged explosion and the attendant crisis. In fact, a number of researchers and commentators are even questioning the very idea of a litigation explosion.

Stephen Daniels, *The Judges' Journal*, Spring 1985.

Alternative dispute resolution is not a new concept at all. What is new is the adaptation or "annexation," if you will, of alternative dispute processing to the federal district courts. . . .

Many lawyers are aware of the court-annexed arbitration experiment conducted beginning in 1978 in the Eastern District of Pennsylvania, the District of Connecticut and the Northern District of California and evaluated by the Federal Judicial Center. That experiment involved mandatory, non-binding arbitration before a panel of three arbitrators in cases seeking money damages not exceeding $100,000 and consisting principally of personal injury or contract subject matter.

The evaluation has produced evidence that the arbitration employed by those courts generally caused a decrease in time from filing to disposition of cases. It also was found that arbitration produced a stimulus to settlement. Because of these results, the Northern District of Illinois has formed a committee of judges and lawyers, of which I am a member, which is currently considering the development of a local rule on mandatory arbitration patterned somewhat after the rules in those three districts. . . .

The Eastern District of Michigan adopted a local rule in 1981 permitting a judge to refer diversity jurisdiction cases to a mediation panel and to impose certain costs as a penalty if a resulting trial does not improve on the award suggested by the mediation panel. This mediation project mirrors a similar program that has been functioning successfully in the Michigan state court system for years. The mediation panels are composed of three attorneys: one selected by a representative of the plaintiff bar, one by a representative of the defense bar and a neutral panel member selected by the chief judge of the circuit court. It is my understanding that the judges of that district believe that the program is effective in increasing the likelihood of settlement of diversity cases.

Myths About Lawyers

Over the centuries many things have been said about lawyers, and few have been flattering. Lord Brougham described a lawyer as a "learned gentleman who rescues your estate from your enemies and keeps it himself." Jeremy Bentham, an eminent 19th-century British political scientist, said that "lawyers are the only persons in whom ignorance of the law is not punished."

These perceptions persist today among the general public. One myth about lawyers, however, must be dislodged. That myth is that "all lawyers are contentious, litigious, and therefore are not amenable to alternatives to litigation." The truth is that most lawyers are in favor of negotiated settlements for disputes, with or without intervention of third parties. A small percentage of litigators and a small percentage of obstinate clients account for the misperception of litigiousness that has been attributed to lawyers as a group by the press and the reading public. There may be other reasons why lawyers resist mediation—for instance, confidentiality problems or limitation on attorneys' fees—but it isn't a litigation mindset. To understand this phenomenon, one has to understand the nature and scope of the universe of disputes in this country.

Galanter describes the universe of all disputes as a dispute "pyramid." The vast portion of the lower part of the pyramid consists of a practically limitless sea of events, collisions, rivalries, disappointments and injuries. Most disputes drawn from this sea are resolved by negotiation between the parties without third party intervention. Some disputes are heard in some formal "forum" in a social setting—for example, before a school principal, shop steward or administrator.

Some disputes move up in levels within the pyramid, transforming, expanding and often becoming more complex as they go. Lawyers often are viewed as important agents of this transformation process. They help translate clients' disputes into applicable legal categories. Lawyers also act as gatekeepers, screening out non-meritorious claims. As the stakes increase, so does the resort to third parties.

Litigation in Only a Few Cases

Litigation actually occurs in a very tiny percentage of all disputes, and it usually happens where there is no anticipated future relationship, business or personal, between the parties. Even in litigation, most lawyers constantly seek ways to settle differences between the parties. The higher the stakes involved and the greater the polarization of the parties, the less is the trust that exists between the litigants, and the more remote the possibilities of settlement become. Having no other recourse, lawyers generally are stuck on the litigation track, steaming to an expensive unknown destination.

Shunting this litigation to an alternative course can greatly diminish the length and expense of the journey. Once the litigation has achieved top momentum, however, it is difficult to convince attorneys of the value of mediation. What emerges from this analysis, however, is that in general attorneys are not overlitigious or contentious. They generally favor resolution of disputes short of adjudication, because that is usually in the best interest of their clients. Attorneys are not necessarily the culprits who encourage litigation, but they are often the victim of circumstances.

"The proposals to cut off attorneys' fees, to limit or abolish punitive and pain-and-suffering damages . . . will only encourage industry and individuals to continue to cause harm."

Liability Suits Protect the Consumer

Miles W. Lord

Miles W. Lord is a former US district judge who, throughout his career, remained controversial for his outspoken opinions. One of his most famous and controversial decisions involved finding the makers of the Dalkon Shield contraceptive criminally liable for the reproductive damage it caused to thousands of women. In the following viewpoint, Lord argues that liability suits are the only insurance many people have against huge and irresponsible corporations. Any action taken to limit access to the courts would mean a curtailment of consumer protection.

As you read, consider the following questions:

1. Why does the author criticize the insurance industry?
2. Why does Lord believe that penalizing a corporation with a heavy punitive damage award protects the consumer?
3. Why must corporations remain financially responsible to the consumer, according to the author?

Miles W. Lord, "Don't Rob Consumers of Their Best Defense," *Minneapolis Star and Tribune,* September 7, 1986. Reprinted by permission of the Minneapolis Star and Tribune.

Minnesota and the nation are seeing a massive attack against our legal system and the methods developed over hundreds of years to compensate injured people. Much of this criticism comes from the insurance industry, which is raising premiums and canceling coverage for many businesses and activities. Rather than accept responsibility for the bad business decisions that have fueled this "insurance crisis," insurance companies have spent millions (of policyholders' money) in an attempt to redefine the problem as a "lawsuit crisis."

Insurance companies seek to reduce their risks through regulation, and in some cases elimination, of the individual's right to recover for injuries caused by another.

Yet at the same time the industry has been successful in opposing any federal regulation and almost all state regulation of its affairs. It is the only major industry exempt from major provisions of the antitrust laws. It receives generous and preferential federal income-tax treatment by being able to deduct losses not yet paid. It refuses to report, in any meaningful detail, its investment income, expenses, capital gains and the relationship between the premiums collected and the amount of losses eventually paid.

Insurance Industry Is Profitable

Yet we know it is profitable. The insurance industry has consistently outperformed the Standard and Poors 500 and the New York Stock Exchange composite over the past 10 years and has continued to pay dividends to shareholders, even in recent "bad" times. Investors know that insurance companies make money. According to a report issued by the U.S. General Accounting Office, total gains for the property-casualty insurance industry nationwide from 1975 to 1984 amounted to more than $72 billion, while the industry's taxes were a *negative* $63 million.

Other industries, which also decry the "lawsuit crisis," would like government "off their backs," too. Industry has been particularly successful in its efforts to control agencies of the state and federal government whose duty it is to protect consumers. Victims discovered long ago that they could not look to these agencies for protection, so they turned to the courts.

In the past 25 years it has been my experience that the government does not protect the public from injury, but that jury verdicts do influence the types of goods manufactured and sold—by making awards that discourage further offenses. The victim of previous wrongs is used as a vehicle to punish and deter further wrongs.

In the '50s and early '60s, millions of women took DES, a drug that was supposed to prevent miscarriages. It was later determined that hundreds of thousands of babies suffered birth defects and, later on, cancer of the reproductive organs. When this case is multiplied by many thousands of people, the enormity of the wrong committed by one small segment of the pharmaceutical industry is evident. These companies must be forced to test their products adequately before marketing them. A heavy punitive damage award is a strong incentive to ensure safer products. Is it unfair to ask for compensation for never being able to have a normal family life, for the inability to bear a child, for the anxiety and disconsolateness of a broken marriage?

Countless Lives Saved

The law of products liability providing that a manufacturer of dangerous products is liable to the reasonably foreseeable users of those products was developed through litigation. Automobiles, airplanes, and many other products have been made safer and countless lives and limbs saved as a result of vigorous litigation.

Lois G. Forer, *Money and Justice*, 1984.

The insurance companies and some industries express shock and dismay when an injured victim rises up from his sickbed and asks for just compensation. Rather than producing safe and effective drugs and machinery, industries complain that it is becoming too expensive to do business.

Thus the insurance industry proposes legislation to limit damages for pain and suffering. The industry also proposes to limit the pay for attorneys representing the injured. It does not propose to limit the compensation of its own lawyers, who are paid with the victims' insurance premiums and who do everything possible to defeat the injured person's claims.

Attorneys Protect Consumers

Attorneys representing injured victims are the only effective consumer protection against the predatory and callous acts of many businesses. Injured people simply cannot afford to hire lawyers by the hour or day. They must obtain lawyers who agree to help them and collect their fee only from the "winnings," if any. Their key to the courthouse is a lawyer's agreement to take a case on a contingent-fee basis.

It has been suggested that the most effective way of dealing with personal injury and product liability would be to remove these areas from the adversarial system. Instead, a social-injury insurance fund would be created. Someone (those self-serving government agencies?) would determine what constitutes an injury and what an injury is worth. The costs would then be passed on to the public through insurance premiums.

This proposal has three major flaws. First, the determination of what an injury is and how much it is worth would present major difficulties. If the responsibility for making these decisions were transferred from a jury to a government agency, this determination would no longer be a social issue but, instead, political. The value of a severed leg should not fluctuate depending upon whether Democrats or Republicans are in office.

Individuals Would Pay

Second, it would essentially require all taxpayers to shoulder the financial burden of the errors of a particular industry. The responsibility and accountability for harm done would be transferred to the proposed insurance system. If someone makes a profit from dispensing drugs that poison or from selling machines and devices that kill, should the taxpayer pay the victims' bills and thus subsidize such misconduct?

More important, however, is the fact that if industry and individuals are no longer financially responsible for their negligence and misconduct, the only proven effective means of deterring such conduct will be lost. In essence, this proposal gives industry license to maim and kill without having to pay the bill.

Continued Harm

Insurance premiums are out of line; the blame has been placed on the legal system. The insurance industry, however, should set its own house in order. It has engaged in selfish and shortsighted business practices. The recent mistreatment of physicians, chiropractors, public agencies and business through raising their premiums to unconscionable levels is a ploy to enlist the aid of these people and institutions in passing bad legislation. These proposals to cut off attorneys' fees, to limit or abolish punitive and pain-and-suffering damages and perhaps even to implement social insurance will only encourage industry and individuals to continue to cause harm.

"As a people we must somehow get over the notion that the solution to every problem is a lawsuit."

Liability Suits Harm the Consumer

Ernest Conine

Ernest Conine is a *Los Angeles Times* editorial writer. In the following viewpoint, he argues that the cost of enormous jury awards now given out in criminal liability suits harms only one segment of the population: the consumer. It is the consumer, he argues, that must eventually pay in the form of higher insurance and medical bills, and lost employment opportunities from companies who can no longer afford to stay in business.

As you read, consider the following questions:

1. Why does the author believe that the current attitude about insurance companies is misguided?
2. What kind of change is required of the public, according to the author?
3. After reading this viewpoint and that of Lord, who would you argue is more convincing?

Just as you don't have to be an artist to know what you like and don't like, you don't have to be a lawyer to conclude that something is terribly wrong with the civil-justice system. Especially the personal- and product-liability branches.

The country has gone sue-crazy.

It is hard to pick up a newspaper without reading that somebody is suing somebody else for $1 million, $50 million or $1 billion. Of course filing a lawsuit is one thing, and collecting is another. But court awards of mind-boggling (and mouth-watering) size are no longer rare.

No one in his right mind would argue against the principle involved in personal- and product-liability cases. If a surgeon removes the wrong organ, he (or his insurer) should foot the bill for his carelessness. People who are injured by a defective product are entitled to collect for their pain and lost earnings.

Room for Common Sense

Surely, though, there is room for common sense. Before handing out sky-is-the-limit awards, frequently on the most esoteric findings of fault, judges and juries should ponder the effect on the world outside the courtroom.

The prevailing attitude was reflected in a conversation among friends of this writer who heard an item on the evening news about a big judgment awarded to a man injured in a collision with a truck.

Everybody agreed that, based on the facts as reported, the jury seemed to have gone overboard. But, as one fellow said, "Oh, well, why not give the guy a break? The insurance company can afford it."

Entirely overlooked is the fact that in the real world it isn't just the insurance company that pays. We all pay in the form of higher premiums for our own insurance or, more important, in higher prices passed along by businesses whose insurance costs keep going up and up. In some cases it becomes uneconomic to provide the product or service at all.

Liability Insurance Costs

To take an easy example, back in 1962 the cost of liability insurance and associated legal activities accounted for only 0.25% of the selling price of a small aircraft. Today, although the safety record of such airplanes is no worse than before, liability-related costs range from 10% to 30% of the sale price at Cessna. The experience of other manufacturers is similar.

One reason is that the manufacturers remain at risk for all the

By Gamble for the Florida Times-Union. Reprinted with permission.

aircraft that they have ever built—going back to 1927 in the case of Cessna. Another is the "deep-pockets" approach to compensation that has been adopted by the courts.

Say the court finds that in the crash of a rental plane 25% of the fault was attributed to pilot error, 60% to the rental company and only 15% to the manufacturer. Yet the manufacturer may be stuck with practically the whole bill on the ground that his financial resources are greater.

The result has been thousands of lost jobs in Kansas and Florida as the price of small aircraft, swollen by the manufacturer's higher insurance costs, soared into the stratosphere. And the same legal principles apply to manufacturers of more down-to-earth products.

It remains to be seen what the courts will decide about the chemical accident at Bhopal, which caused more than 2,000 deaths. But the fallout is already being felt by firms that have nothing to do with the case or the type of chemical involved.

Costs of Handling Hazardous Chemicals

The cost of liability insurance for firms that handle hazardous chemicals or wastes is up by 75%, to 500%. Many are finding it difficult to get coverage at any price.

Chemical manufacturers fear that they will be stuck for the misdeeds of industrial users of their products. As one industry expert told *Industry Week*, "Any lawyer will tell you that the 'deep-pockets' theory says that you go after the guy with the most money." And the ultimate cost will be paid by the ordinary consumer.

Then take the medical field, where malpractice suits have mushroomed in recent years. The result is a sharp rise in liability-insurance rates, passed on to patients in most cases, plus a trend toward expensive tests and procedures conducted primarily to defend against possible malpractice charges. In New York state alone such "defensive" medicine adds an estimated $2 billion a year to health costs.

In the present climate an ordinary homeowner risks being held responsible for injuries to a burglar in the performance of his crime, or for a defect in a house that was sold years before. Any Californian who doesn't buy the maximum available auto-liability insurance is flirting with ruin.

A Glendale, California judge recently ruled against a couple who accused a church of clerical malpractice because of advice given to a youth who later committed suicide. But tens of thousands of churches find it prudent to dip into the collection box to pay for insurance against such suits.

I know of no accurate figures for the total cost of the liability system as it now operates, but surely it would come to tens or even hundreds of billions of dollars.

The point is not that the personal- and product-liability system should be dismantled, but that we recognize that compassion must be balanced by concern over the price being paid in terms of higher consumer prices, constrained employment opportunities and ability of U.S. business to compete with foreign producers not similarly encumbered.

Legislative Remedies

All kinds of corrective actions have been suggested, including statutory limits on injury awards, reform of the contingency-fee system that encourages lawyers to pursue even frivolous cases, and more frequent use of the judicial power to impose financial penalties on losing plaintiffs.

One suspects, though, that legislative remedies are less important than getting our heads straight.

As a people we must somehow get over the notion that the solution to every problem is a lawsuit. Not every illness has a cure. Even well-designed and well-built products will sometimes fail, particularly in the hands of a careless user. Some tragic occurrences are the fault of the people to whom they happen. There never has been, and never can be, a risk-free society.

Most fundamental of all, there is no superfund in the sky from which multi-million-dollar awards are paid. The money can come from only one place: your pocketbook and mine.

"As tort law operates now, it is more like a lottery than like a rational system of justice."

Many Liability Suits Are Unjustified

Michael Kinsley

Michael Kinsley is an editor for *The New Republic*, a weekly opinion magazine. In the following viewpoint, Kinsley argues that liability suits have become ridiculous. Companies are held responsible for the effects of products that have been approved by the government or, in some cases, produced long before the negative effects were known. He concludes by arguing that legislation to cap jury awards and lawyer fees in liability suits is a positive move.

As you read, consider the following questions:

1. What three changes in tort law does the author bemoan?
2. What discrepancies exist in liability settlements, according to Kinsley?
3. What point does the author make about the element of risk in everyone's lives? How does this relate to the liability crisis?

Michael Kinsley, "Craziness in the Courtroom," *The New Republic*, November 18, 1985. Reprinted by permission of THE NEW REPUBLIC, © 1985, The New Republic, Inc.

A Kansas court in 1984 awarded $10 million, including $8 million in punitive damages, to a man who got the polio virus from his daughter after she took the Sabin oral polio vaccine. A jury ruled that it is "outrageous" to sell the Sabin vaccine when the Salk vaccine is safer.

The Salk vaccine *is* safer. The Sabin is a live but weakened virus that causes about 10 polio cases a year out of some 20 million doses, while the Salk, made from dead viruses, cannot cause polio. On the other hand, the Sabin is more effective for use in the United States, according to national medical-advisory committees. Ten or so Americans a year get polio now, compared with several thousand a year during the era when the Salk was the only vaccine. The Sabin's contribution to this trend, among other reasons, is why it is official U.S. policy to prefer it. But if the Kansas case becomes a precedent, there is a strong possibility that no drug company will make the Sabin vaccine.

When people fret about unelected judges making important social policy, they usually have in mind the Supreme Court's rulings about the Constitution. But another kind of judicial activism is coming to have an equal or greater effect on life in America. That is the explosion, set off primarily by state courts, in tort law— civil suits arising out of alleged misconduct or negligence. Fear of lawsuits and inability to get insurance are affecting drug companies, municipalities, corporate directors, doctors and others as surely as if the government had issued new laws or regulations. Many of these judge-made "regulations," which have been percolating through the legal system over the past two decades, are ones no sane government would consider.

Inability To Take Action

The coming tort crisis is one example of a major problem of modern American government: our inability to take action for the general public good if it harms identifiable individuals. Trade protectionism, tax loopholes and overgenerous entitlements are all part of the same dilemma. But courts add their own special madness. They make decisions involving complex policy issues about which they have little expertise. They are institutionally inclined to focus on the costs of whatever behavior they have under scrutiny, without regard to the benefits.

Under our federal-state system, the same issue can be litigated again and again across the land, with similar or opposite results. However, since the plaintiffs tend to be local and the defendants are often out-of-state corporations able to afford large settlements, there is an inevitable tendency to follow the lead of states that have been the most aggressive in finding liability.

The idea of tort law is that if my misbehavior causes you harm, I should pay you money to make up for it. Plaintiffs' trial lawyers have worked wonders to expand the concept in recent years. Punitive damages—payments beyond all compensation for actual loss, intended to punish the defendant—are far more common then they once were. Courts have become far more imaginative in their definitions of actual harm as well, awarding large sums for emotional distress, fear of getting cancer (as opposed to actually getting cancer) and so on. Where it is impossible to know whether the defendant's activity actually caused the plaintiff's harm—did the victim get cancer from living downwind of a nuclear testing site or just by chance?—some courts have held that defendants must prove they *aren't* responsible.

Reprinted with permission.

But the biggest advances have been made in dispensing with the notion that you must have done something wrong in order to be held liable. No human endeavor is risk-free. If you can't be accused of failing to eliminate all risk, you can be accused of "failure to warn" of the risk that remains.

The first successful suit against the Sabin vaccine, in 1968, turned on the manufacturer's failure to warn recipients of the infinitesimal chance of catching polio from it. More and more, though, any pretense of finding fault is abandoned, and manufacturers of inevitably risky products are held totally responsible for any harm that comes from them. It is no defense that your product or activity is approved by the government agency that supervises such things. A chemical company recently was held liable for "mislabeling" a can of the paraquat herbicide (a poison), even though the wording used was *expressly approved* by the Environmental Protection Agency.

Fear of juries has led defendants to settle suits, whatever their merits. High settlements have contributed significantly to skyrocketing insurance rates. The "tax" that pays for this is huge, but hidden ($4.50 for a dose of diphtheria vaccine that cost 11 cents a few years ago), so there is little political resistance.

Members of the Reagan Administration who are alarmed about the trend regard it resentfully as back-door government activism. In an era when new regulatory agencies and new social-welfare programs don't have a prayer through normal democratic channels, they see liberal judges and tort lawyers conjuring up vast schemes for income redistribution and controls on business through the courts.

Tort Law Lottery

But liberals should also be alarmed by the tort explosion. As tort law operates now, it is more like a lottery than like a rational system of justice. Yes, some sufferers receive the balm of money. But people with the identical grievance can collect radically different amounts. What you collect depends on such factors as where you live, the assets of the defendant, what judge you get and the amount of your lost earnings. This means that affluent people—who are more likely to sue in the first place—often collect more than poor people do for the same grievance.

And much of the income redistribution caused by tort cases is from everyone else to the lawyers—if you include what the defendants' lawyers get paid. For instance, according to a Rand Corporation study, in all the current litigation over asbestos, the average cost to the defendant has been $101,000. Of that, $37,000 has gone to the defendant's lawyers, $25,000 to the plaintiff's lawyers, and $39,000 is left for the plaintiff.

Worst of all, the tort system teaches a cramped lesson about justice and injustice. Most of the suffering in our society is part of everyday life. Relief from suffering needn't depend on finding someone to blame. The instinct that says it's wrong for people to suffer unnecessarily should be directed into politics, not into lawsuits.

A number of solutions have been proposed to the problems of state courts' competing against one another with ever-wackier theories of tort liability. One is that national legislation should set sensible rules, and exempt from the risk of lawsuits those activities that meet federal standards.

Some Winners in the Torts Lottery

• A man had a heart attack while trying to start a lawn mower. In a suit against the manufacturer, he argued that pulling the starter rope required excessive effort. A jury awarded him $1 million in damages—plus interest. (To avoid further litigation, the company settled the case out of court.)

• An Oregon jury ordered Ford to pay $1.5 million to the estate of a woman who was killed when a runaway horse she hit crashed through the roof of her Ford Pinto. Although Ford argued that the case was "one in a million" and no car could withstand such an impact, the jury found the auto maker liable. (Ford is appealing the decision.)

• An intoxicated California driver lost control of her car and veered into a telephone booth, injuring the man inside. Suit was brought in superior court against the companies responsible for the design, location, installation and maintenance of the booth. Then the state supreme court ruled that a jury should be permitted to find these defendants liable, and it was of no consequence that the harm was caused by an intoxicated driver. (The case was settled out of court for an undisclosed amount.)

• New York City settled out of court and paid $650,000 to a man mutilated when he tried to commit suicide by jumping in front of a subway train. He claimed the driver was partially responsible for not stopping sooner.

Reader's Digest, May 1986.

Assistant Attorney General Richard K. Willard recommends other changes. "Solutions might include caps on the amounts for pain and suffering and other noneconomic damages, and limitations on punitive damages," he says. "We must also give serious thought to limiting attorneys' fees—assuring that liability judgments go to the injured, not to attorneys' pockets. In short, we must rein in the runaway tort system and bring its costs under control."

"It turns out that jurors weren't quite so silly as the anecdotes make them sound. It turns out that if you had been on the jury you might have voted for the plaintiff."

Liability Suits Are Justified

Tom Braden

Seemingly irrational liability suits are regularly publicized in the national media. These suits have made most people wonder whether legislative controls on jury awards are necessary. In the following viewpoint, Tom Braden, a nationally-syndicated columnist, argues that these much-publicized stories have another, more rational side. In each of the cases he cites, he shows that the litigants did indeed have a legitimate case.

As you read, consider the following questions:

1. Why isn't the author sympathetic to insurance companies that must pay large jury awards?
2. Braden makes a general point on why these particular cases were justified. What is it?

Tom Braden, "Insurance Horror Stories," *The Washington Times*, April 4, 1986. Reprinted with the author's permission.

We hear a lot of horror stories. There's the one about the guy who entered a race carrying a 400-pound refrigerator on his back.

He fell and was injured and sued the producers of the race for a million dollars. He won.

There's the one that interested the president. A man was pulling the cord on his power lawn mower, suffered a heart attack, and sued the manufacturer for a million dollars. He settled out of court for an undisclosed but substantial sum.

There's the one about the horse hitting the Pinto. That's *Green* vs. *Ford Motor Co.* Mr. Green was driving at night when a horse ambled out of a field and onto the road. He hit the horse, which went straight into the air and came down on the roof, collapsing it. He sued, for a million and a half, and won.

All these stories and others are cited as examples of the tremendous awards that juries are mistakenly handing out to people who take the trouble to sue. The result, say the storytellers, is that the insurance companies are going broke, and the president has to come to their aid with proposals which would put a stop or a ceiling on the silly and expensive awards.

Finding the Opposite Side

But when you look into the stories you find there is another side. That man who entered a race carrying a 400-pound refrigerator was a world champion bodybuilder. He was given a written contract testifying that all the equipment had been tested for safety. The trial proved that it had not been tested, and that in fact the chief engineer had warned producers of the race—televised on CBS—that he didn't think the equipment was safe.

The man who had a heart attack trying to start the lawn mower proved in court that the lawn mower was defective according to the manufacturer's own specifications. It would not have started if he had pulled the starter rope from now until he died a natural death.

The story of the Green family is a sad one. Mr. Green was driving his wife home from the hospital where she had just been delivered of a baby. She was struck on the temple when the roof collapsed under the weight of the horse and was killed. Mr. Green proved in court that the Pinto's roof could not withstand the 5,000 pounds of pressure specified by the National Transportation Safety Board and that the company's records of vehicles which failed this test had been destroyed.

So it turns out that jurors weren't quite so silly as the anecdotes make them sound. It turns out that if you had been on the jury you might have voted for the plaintiff. Most important, it turns out that the plaintiff either had a contract (in the case of the weight lifter) or a presumption of product safety.

There's no doubt Americans are suing and recovering for what we used to accept as accidents. There were 1,579 product-safety suits in 1975 and 10,745 in 1984. But is this altogether a bad thing? Doesn't the threat of lawsuits exert a discipline on manufacturers, forcing them to obey laws, follow regulations, inspect products? Might we not otherwise experience a lot more "pain and suffering" than we do now?

Litigation and Corporate Conscience

Civil litigation has . . . been instrumental in improving the environment, promoting safety, and protecting consumers from a wide variety of daily hazards. It was a lawsuit that compelled the Reserve Mining Company to stop dumping asbestos waste into Lake Superior and to pay for filtering the water used by the residents of Duluth, Minnesota. The flood of suits against the asbestos mining and manufacturing companies, by workmen injured and dying from exposure to asbestos and by the relatives of those already dead, has forced the discontinuance of the use of asbestos in ships, school buildings, office buildings, and many other places. Litigation or the fear of litigation has compelled auto manufacturers to recall thousands of defective machines that could have caused injury or death to the drivers and passengers, other motorists, and pedestrians. Had these cars not been recalled, the ensuing accidents would have given rise to many cases brought by car owners and victims of accidents. Experience has shown that when litigation becomes sufficiently costly, industry revises its practices and improves its products. Litigation is the spur to an enlightened corporate conscience.

Lois G. Forer, *Money and Justice*, 1984.

As for the insurance problem, the companies lowered premiums several years ago in a price war which turned into a disaster. They counted on investing their money at high interest rates for their profits. When the interest rates went down, they were wounded, and they now are trying to heal their wounds by raising the rates again.

Recognizing Statements That Are Provable

From various sources of information we are constantly confronted with statements and generalizations about social and moral problems. In order to think clearly about these problems, it is useful if one can make a basic distinction between statements for which evidence can be found and other statements which cannot be verified or proved because evidence is not available, or the issue is so controversial that it cannot be definitely proved.

Readers should be aware that magazines, newspapers, and other sources often contain statements of a controversial nature. The following activity is designed to allow experimentation with statements that are provable and those that are not.

Most of the following statements are taken from the viewpoints in the fourth chapter of this book. Consider each statement carefully. *Mark P for any statement you believe is provable. Mark U for any statement you feel is unprovable because of the lack of evidence. Mark C for any statements you think are too controversial to be proved to everyone's satisfaction.*

If you are doing this activity as a member of a class or group, compare your answers with those of other class or group members. Be able to defend your answers. You may discover that others will come to different conclusions than you. Listening to the reasons others present for their answers may give you valuable insights in recognizing statements that are provable.

If you are reading this book alone, ask others if they agree with your answers. You too will find this interaction valuable.

P = provable
U = unprovable
C = too controversial

1. Most liability suits are totally unjustified.

2. Insurance companies would like to reduce their business risks by regulating the individual's right to sue.

3. In England, losing parties must pay the cost of litigation.

4. The chemical disaster at Bhopal caused more than 2,000 deaths.

5. The insurance industry's mistreatment of doctors and businesses through raising their premiums to absurd levels is a ploy to enlist the aid of these people and institutions in passing bad legislation to curtail litigation.

6. Much of the damage award from lawsuits goes to lawyers, which is why they are so eager to sue.

7. The insurance industry receives preferential income-tax treatment by being able to deduct losses not yet paid.

8. Liability suits are the only way to make careless, irresponsible businesses make their products safer.

9. The fact that Americans are extremely litigious cannot be disputed.

10. Approximately 88 percent of all civil cases filed in American courts are settled.

11. A few overly zealous litigators and a small percentage of obstinate clients account for the myth that lawyers are overly litigious.

12. It is a myth that America is experiencing a "litigation explosion" in its trial courts.

13. The insurance industry has consistently outperformed the New York Stock Exchange composite over the past 10 years.

14. Any Californian who doesn't buy the maximum available auto liability insurance is flirting with ruin.

15. The Pinto roof which collapsed under the weight of a horse could not withstand the 5,000 pounds of pressure specified by the National Transportation Safety Board.

16. The government does not protect the public from injury, but jury verdicts, which punish negligent manufacturers, do influence the type of goods manufactured and sold and thus may protect consumers.

17. The DES drug, which was supposed to prevent miscarriages, in fact caused birth defects.

Periodical Bibliography

The following list of periodical articles deals with the subject matter of this chapter.

Harry S. Ashton — "A Plea for Justice, Not Litigation," *Vital Speeches of the Day*, March 1983.

Michael Brody — "Litigation and Insurance," *Current*, July/August 1986.

Michael Galanter — "America's Litigation Binge Is a Myth," *U.S. News & World Report*, November 19, 1984.

Ted Gest — "Sky-High Damage Suits," *U.S. News & World Report*, January 27, 1986.

Ted Gest — "Soaring Legal Costs: Even Lawyers Are Worried," *U.S. News & World Report*, August 13, 1984.

Richard R. Korn — "Litigation Can Be Therapeutic," *Corrections Magazine*, October 1981.

William M. Landes and A. Posner — "New Light on Punitive Damages," *Regulation*, September/October 1986.

Stanley J. Lieberman — "A No-Lose Proposition," *Newsweek*, February 21, 1983.

Jane Bryant Quinn — "Cutting Back Verdicts," *Newsweek*, July 7, 1986.

Jay Stuller — "Runaway Law: Our Litigious Society," *The American Legion*, March 1983.

William L. Taylor — "Litigation as an Empowerment Tool," *Social Policy*, Spring 1986.

U.S. News & World Report — "Where People Are Most Litigious," August 18, 1986.

William Wallace — "The Expanding Cost of Tort Litigation," *Vital Speeches of the Day*, November 15, 1985.

Richard K. Willard — "Wheel of Fortune," *Policy Review*, Spring 1986.

Nicholas C. Yost — "Don't Further Weaken Citizens' Lawsuits," *The New York Times*, November 12, 1983.

Do the Rights of the Accused Undermine the Criminal Justice System?

"Is a society redeemed if it provides massive safeguards for accused persons . . . yet fails to provide elementary protection for its law-abiding citizens?"

The Legal System Gives Too Much Protection to Criminals

Warren E. Burger

Warren E. Burger is the former chief justice of the US Supreme Court. Known for his strict attitudes toward punishing the accused, he remained a controversial figure during his years in the court. In the following viewpoint, Burger argues that the rights of the accused have dismantled the criminal justice system and allowed the guilty to go free.

As you read, consider the following questions:

1. What evidence does the author present to support his claim that crime has almost paralyzed society?
2. What is the core of any effective response to crime, according to Burger?
3. How does the author believe that the criminal justice system encourages offenders to fight society?

Warren E. Burger, speech delivered to the American Bar Association in Houston, Texas on February 8, 1981.

Crime and the fear of crime has permeated the fabric of American life, damaging the poor and minorities even more than the affluent. A recent survey indicates forty-six percent of women and forty-eight percent of Negroes are "significantly frightened" by pervasive crime in America. . . .

We are all victims of crime. . . .

We are approaching the status of an impotent society—a society whose capability of maintaining elementary security on the streets, in schools, and for the homes of our people is in doubt. . . .

We have established a system of criminal justice that provides more protection, more safeguards, more guarantees for those accused of crime than any other nation in all history. The protective armor we give to each individual when the State brings a charge is great indeed. . . .

Rights of Accused Harm Society

I put to you this question: Is a society redeemed if it provides massive safeguards for accused persons including pretrial freedom for most crimes, defense lawyers at public expense, trials, and appeals, re-trials and more appeals—almost without end—and yet fails to provide elementary protection for its law-abiding citizens? I ask you to ponder this question as you hear me out.

Time does not allow—not does my case require—that I burden you with masses of detailed statistics—I assure you the statistics are not merely grim, they are frightening. Let me begin near home: Washington, D.C., the capital of our enlightened country, in 1980 had more criminal homicides than Sweden and Denmark combined with an aggregate population of over twelve million as against 650,000 for Washington, D.C. and Washington is not unique. From New York City, to Los Angeles, to Miami the story on increase in violent crime from 1979 to 1980 is much the same. New York City with about the same population as Sweden has 20 times as many homicides. The United States has one hundred times the rate of burglary of Japan. Overall violent crime in the United States increased sharply from 1979 to 1980, continuing a double-digit rate. More than one-quarter of all the households in this country are victimized by some kind of criminal activity at least once each year. . . .

What the American people want is that crime and criminals be brought under control so that we can be safe on the streets and in our homes and for our children to be safe in schools and at play. . . .

Nothing will bring about swift changes in the terror that stalks

*"Your best bet is to plead guilty to everything
and let the legal system set you* free!"

© Leed/Rothco

our streets and endangers our homes, but I will make a few
suggestions. . . .

There is a startling amount of crime committed by persons on
release awaiting trial, on parole, and on probation release. It is
not uncommon for an accused to finally be brought to trial with
two, three or more charges pending. Overburdened prosecutors
and courts tend to drop other pending charges when one conviction is obtained. Should we be surprised if the word gets around
in the "criminal community" that you can commit two or three
crimes for the price of only one and that there is not much risk
in committing crimes while awaiting trial?

Punish the Criminals

Deterrence is the primary core of any effective response to the
reign of terror in American cities. Deterrence means speedy action by society, but that process runs up against the reality that

many large cities have either reduced their police forces or failed to keep them in balance with double-digit crime inflation.

A first step to achieve deterrence is to have larger forces of better trained officers. Thanks to the F.B.I. Academy we have the pattern for such training.

A second step is to re-examine statutes on pre-trial release at every level. This requires that there be a sufficient number of investigators, prosecutors, and defenders—and judges—to bring defendants to trial swiftly. Any study of the statistics will reveal that "bail crime" reflects a great hole in the fabric of protection against internal terrorism.

To change this melancholy picture will call for spending more money than we have ever before devoted to law enforcement, and even this will be for naught if we do not re-examine our judicial process and philosophy with respect to finality of judgments. The search for "perfect" justice has led us on a course found nowhere else in the world. . . .

Technical Errors Release Criminals

Our search for true justice must not be twisted into an endless quest for technical errors unrelated to guilt or innocence. . . .

Governments were instituted and exist chiefly to protect people. If governments fail in this basic duty they are not excused, they are not redeemed by showing that they have established the most perfect system to protect the claims of defendants in criminal cases. A government that fails to protect both the rights of accused persons and also all other people has failed in its mission. I leave it to you whether the balance has been fairly struck. . . .

Many enlightened countries succeed in holding criminal trials within four to eight weeks after arrest. First non-violent offenders are generally placed on probation, free to return to a gainful occupation under close supervision. But I hardly need to remind this audience that our criminal process often goes on two, three, four or more years before the accused runs out of all the options. Even after sentence and confinement, the warfare continues with endless streams of petitions for writs, suits against parole boards, wardens and judges.

Constant Warfare with Society

So we see a paradox—even while we struggle toward correction, education and rehabilitation of the offender, our system encourages prisoners to continue warfare with society. The result is that whatever may have been the defendant's hostility toward the police, the witnesses, the prosecutors, the judge and jurors—and the public defender who failed to win his case—those hostilities are kept alive. How much chance do you think there is of changing or rehabilitating a person who is encouraged to keep up years of constant warfare with society?

105

The dismal failure of our system to stem the flood of crime repeaters is reflected in part in the massive number of those who go in and out of prisons. In a nation that has been thought to be the world leader in so many areas of human activity our system of justice—not simply the prisons—produces the world's highest rate of "recall" for those who are processed through it. How long can we tolerate this rate of recall and the devastation it produces? . . .

Safeguarding Society

Now turn with me to a few steps which ought to be considered:

(1) Restore to all pretrial release laws the crucial element of dangerousness to the community based on a combination of the evidence then available and the defendant's past record, to deter crime-while-on-bail;

(2) Provide for trial within weeks of arrest for most cases, except for extraordinary cause shown;

(3) Priority for review on appeal within eight weeks of a judgment of guilt;

(4) Following exhaustion of appellate review, confine all subsequent judicial review to claims of miscarriage of justice;

and finally:

A. We must accept the reality that to confine offenders behind walls without trying to change them is an expensive folly with short term benefits—a "winning of battles while losing the war";

The Criminals Are Winning

Years on the bench punctuated by countless bond forfeitures and probation revocations have persuaded me that *the criminals are winning.* While we in the black robes were trying to apply the law in a humane and rehabilitative manner, the thieves and bullies were laughing at us. In all probability, our well-intentioned efforts to provide a "second chance" have encouraged more criminals to commit more crimes.

Charles L. Weltner, *Atlanta Weekly,* May 2, 1982.

B. Provide for generous use of probation for first non-violent offenders, with intensive supervision and counseling and swift revocation if probation terms are violated;

C. A broad scale program of physical rehabilitation of the penal institutions to provide a decent setting for expanded educational and vocational training;

D. Make all vocational and educational programs mandatory with credit against the sentence for educational progress—literally a program to "learn the way out of prison," so that no prisoner leaves without at least being able to read, write, do basic arithmetic and have a marketable skill;

E. Generous family visitation in decent surroundings to maintain family ties, with rigid security to exclude drugs or weapons;

F. Counseling services after release paralleling the "after-care" services in Sweden, Holland, Denmark, and Finland. All this should be aimed at developing the prisoner's respect for self, respect for others, accountability for conduct, and appreciation of the value of work, of thrift, and of family.

G. Encourage religious groups to give counsel on ethical behavior and occupational adjustment during and after confinement.

"These carefully enunciated [criminal] rights, won after many years of bitterly fought litigation, are a cruel hoax for the majority of accused persons."

The Legal System Does Not Adequately Protect the Accused

Lois G. Forer

Lois G. Forer has served as a judge of the Court of Common Pleas in Philadelphia since 1971. Judge Forer has served on the Lawyers Committee for Civil Rights under President Kennedy, acted as a consultant to the United States Commission on Civil Disorders, and is the author of several books on criminal justice. In the following viewpoint, she argues that the US criminal justice system provides more safeguards for the accused than any other legal system in the world. However, Forer believes that for the majority of accused persons these laws exist in name only. The system works hopelessly against the poor, many of whom waive their rights and cop a guilty plea on the advice of public defenders who want to dispense with as many cases as possible.

As you read, consider the following questions:

1. According to Forer, why do most poor people never have a trial?
2. Why does the author believe that the guarantee to be represented by a lawyer does not guarantee a fair trial?

Adapted from *Money and Justice, Who Owns the Courts?* by Lois G. Forer. By permission of the author and W.W. Norton & Company, Inc. Copyright © 1984 by Lois G. Forer.

zealously within the bounds of the law and to represent their clients competently, to prepare adequately, and give appropriate attention to the work. A lawyer may not represent a client already represented by another attorney. . . .

Why Worry About the Guilty?

Why, you may wonder, am I worrying about guilty people who have pled guilty? Isn't the legal system supposed to be a search for truth, not a game that lawyers play where anything goes so long as one doesn't break the rules? A guilty plea is not wrong or immoral. If a person has committed an offense and admits it, he should not perjure himself by pleading not guilty, provided that he understands the consequences of the plea and that it is truly voluntary.

Everyone who pleads guilty or gives up his right to trial by jury is supposed to be asked:

Are you doing this of your own free will?

Has anyone threatened or coerced you?

Has anyone promised you anything?

I believe that most judges require that these ritual questions be asked and answered appropriately before accepting a plea. But no one asks whether the accused is coerced economically. Can he afford to wait in jail for trial? Can he afford to track down and subpoena the fact witnesses he needs? Can he afford to retain expert witnesses to examine the physical evidence? . . . How many poor defendants retain an expert to prove that the alleged blood on the defendant's clothing was not blood, but paint? A conviction of murder based on the state's evidence that stains on the defendant's shorts were blood (presumably that of the victim) was set aside when experts proved that the stains were paint, as the defendant had maintained. How many defendants have been convicted on scientifically false testimony that hairs found on the victim's body or clothing were hairs of the defendant? For years prosecutors used such "evidence." The FBI published a leaflet, "Don't Miss a Hair." It is now conceded that no positive identification can be made on the basis of a few hairs. No one will ever know the number of people who were convicted, sentenced, and even executed in felony cases on the basis of false and unreliable evidence. . . .

I must question . . . whether the nominal rights accorded under our criminal justice system are a matter of conscience or convenience. The courts conveniently dispose of 90 percent of criminal cases swiftly, legally, and without challenge because they have complied with the prescribed ritual. But conscience compels one to admit that although the forms of justice have been meticulously followed, the substance of equal protection of the laws is routinely denied to many poor persons accused of crime.

113

"Miranda *turns out to be the police officer's friend.*"

The *Miranda* Rule Has Not Affected Law Enforcement

Patrick Malone

In 1966 the Supreme Court ruled in *Miranda v. Arizona* that police officers must inform apprehended suspects of their legal rights, including the right to remain silent until they have spoken with an attorney. The ruling has remained controversial. Many argue that it undermines police officers' ability to gain confessions. In the following viewpoint, Patrick Malone, a trial lawyer and writer in Washington, DC, writes that the *Miranda* ruling has had little, if any effect, on the police. The psychological training police receive to solicit confessions and the natural tendency of criminals to confess make the *Miranda* ruling little more than rhetoric, he states.

As you read, consider the following questions:

1. What are some of the reasons criminals confess, according to the author?
2. What evidence does the author give to affirm his belief that *Miranda* has not affected the confession rate?
3. Why does Malone believe *Miranda* has failed?

Patrick Malone, "You Have the Right to Remain Silent: Miranda After Twenty Years." Reprinted from THE AMERICAN SCHOLAR, Volume 55, Number 3, Summer 1986. Copyright © 1986 by the author. By permission of the publisher.

Miranda v. Arizona is the only ruling of the United States Supreme Court to add a new verb to the language—to *mirandize* the suspect. When issued twenty years ago, it quickly became—and remains to this day—the most reviled decision ever issued by the Supreme Court in a criminal case. Congressmen called for Chief Justice Earl Warren's impeachment. Constitutional amendments were introduced. Police chiefs predicted chaos. Richard Nixon won the presidency in part by holding up *Miranda* as Exhibit One in the indictment against the excesses of the Warren Court for "coddling criminals" and "hand-cuffing the police."

All this controversy was over a decision that required police departments to do what many law enforcement agencies already practiced: inform a suspect before interrogation of his right not to talk to police and his right to a lawyer—appointed at no cost if he could not afford one—and warn him that, if he did talk, what he said could be used as evidence against him.

Everyone assumed that, once warned of these rights, few suspects would agree to talk to police without a lawyer. The Warren Court's many detractors feared this would paralyze criminal investigations, which relied heavily on obtaining confessions. The Court's few supporters hoped the *Miranda* warnings would reduce the widespread use of trickery and psychologically coercive tactics during police interrogation of suspects. This seemed clearly to be the goal of the majority opinion written by Chief Justice Warren, one that catalogued in damning detail the deceptive practices advocated by leading police procedure manuals and practiced across the country.

Miranda Ineffective

Miranda has met neither side's expectations. The creation of a suspect's right to be told his rights has not appreciably affected the confession rate. Nor has *Miranda* curbed the use by police interrogators of such tactics as showing the suspect fake evidence, putting the suspect to a phony lie detector test that he is guaranteed to flunk, and making fraudulent offers of sympathy and help.

Miranda never was as radical as critics have painted it. The Court in *Miranda* did not ban outright, as it could have, all use of questionable interrogation tactics. Nor did the high court require, as courts in other countries have, that any questioning of a suspect be conducted before a neutral magistrate. Instead, the court formulated what amounted to a warning label as an effort to accommodate ideals of fair play to the perceived necessities of police work. . . .

On closer examination, *Miranda* turns out to be the police officer's friend. The *Miranda* warning has become, in the main, a benediction at the outset of every interrogation, sanctifying the very practices it was meant to end. Studies—in New Haven, Connecticut; Washington, D.C.; Pittsburgh, Pennsylvania; Denver, Colorado; and elsewhere—have found that *Miranda* warnings have little or no effect on a suspect's propensity to talk. Most suspects routinely waive their *Miranda* rights and submit to police questioning. Next to the warning label on cigarette packs, *Miranda* is the most widely ignored piece of official advice in our society. Even when *Miranda* is violated, it is rare that a confession will be ruled inadmissible or that a suspect will go free. Ernest Miranda himself was retried and reconvicted. A recent federally funded study in Illinois, Michigan, and Pennsylvania found that convictions were lost as a result of judges throwing out confessions in only five out of the 7,035 cases studied, or 0.07 percent.

An Important Symbol

Whether suspects do not fully grasp the significance of the warnings, or whether conscience (and the desire to get the matter over with) override the impact of the warnings, it is plain that for the past 20 years suspects have continued to confess with great frequency. It is equally plain that this would not have been the case if Miranda really had projected counsel into the police station. . . .

Clearly, the case is an important symbol. But what follows from that? The police should never forget that they do not establish their own interrogation rules and do not police themselves. As Liva Baker, author of "Miranda: Crime, Law and Politics," has pointed out, the warnings "serve a civilizing purpose"—they remind the police officer that however lowly the suspect before him, he is still a human being possessing certain rights.

Yale Kamisar, *The New York Times,* June 11, 1986.

Most people not closely related to a criminal defendant or a criminal defense lawyer will applaud this news, at least at first blush. The rights of defendants, most of whom richly deserve a spell behind bars, have never been a popular cause, and police tactics have never excited much public curiosity. As the constitutional law scholar Yale Kamisar once observed, the typical police suspect and his interrogator are generally viewed "as garbage and garbage collector, respectively."

But the debate, then and now, is not simply over ritual niceties in police questioning of criminal suspects. It is a debate over what kind of criminal justice system we will have. . . .

It is beyond doubt that the time-honed and sophisticated methods taught by interrogation manuals and police academies are extremely effective in getting suspects to reveal incriminating information—a fact appreciated by few suspects when they sign *Miranda* waiver cards. What is far more uncertain is the frequency with which those statements by suspects are true or false or somewhere in between.

Cases of convincing but false confessions are by their nature difficult to ferret out. Yet they are regularly documented. An eighteen-year-old named Peter Reilly confessed to killing his mother in Canaan, Connecticut. Another young man in Great Britain confessed to raping an eleven-year-old girl. In both cases, the confession seemed credible because it contained facts known only to the police and the real perpetrator. Reilly was freed only after an intense two-year campaign by friends and neighbors that enlisted the sympathy of the playwright Arthur Miller and other celebrities. The British youth was exonerated when it was shown that his blood type differed from that of the attacker. In neither case was the defendant mentally disturbed or otherwise abnormal. Yet the police, using only standard interrogation techniques without any physical threats of violence, persuaded both young men to confess that they were guilty of crimes someone else had committed. . . .

Why Criminals Confess

Why would anyone overstate or falsely state his guilt, especially when the *Miranda* warnings instruct him that anything said will be used against him? The answer requires an exploration of why people confess and how they are led to do so, whether they are guilty or innocent.

From toddler years on, we are taught that confession is both social duty and its own reward. In Christian theology, confession is a key to salvation. The law itself encourages the private expiation of guilt by refusing to require the testimony of those most likely to have heard a criminal defendant's confession—spouse, minister, psychiatrist.

Beyond the ubiquitous social pressure to confess, psychological factors make silence virtually impossible for many people when they are interrogated. A universal rule of polite social discourse is to speak when spoken to. Silence conveys arrogance, hostility, rudeness, and, most of all, guilt. Police interrogators are taught to be careful not to provide an excuse for silence by violating the rules of etiquette. At the same time, they are taught to orchestrate environmental cues with stratagems designed both to lull and to intimidate the suspect into talking.

Training courses advise the interrogator in the style of his or her dress (conservative business suit stripped of any badges or other police identification), the location and decor of the interrogation room (quiet, remote, and bare, with neither reminders that it is in a police station nor with any tension-relieving small objects for the suspect to fiddle with), the seating arrangement (close to the suspect and at eye level), even the desirability of breath mints to avoid losing the psychological advantage of getting physically "next to" the suspect. Taking notes is strictly forbidden. As Fred Inbau and John Reid advise in their classic manual *Criminal Interrogations and Confessions,* "Avoid creating the impression that you are an investigator seeking a confession or conviction.". . .

Miranda and Law Enforcement

In practice few suspects actually rely on their right of silence. Even when the caution that one need not answer is faithfully administered by the interrogating police officer, very few suspects have the strength of mind to say nothing.

In other words, this is an issue on which the realistic right-winger can afford to relax. He can allow the civil libertarians their principled defense of the right of silence, for he knows that most suspects will still talk—and of those who do not, many will nevertheless be convicted. . . .

To a civil libertarian, it seems obviously right and proper that a suspect held in the police station without charges should have early access to a lawyer. Conservatives, on the other hand, worry that lawyers are likely to advise their clients to be silent and otherwise to obstruct police inquiries. But here, too, conservatives ought not to worry—for in fact, most suspects do not ask for a lawyer.

Michael Zander, *The New York Times,* January 27, 1986.

Skillfully presented, the *Miranda* warnings themselves sound chords of fairness and sympathy at the outset of the interrogation. The interrogator who advises, who cautions, who offers the suspect the gift of a free lawyer, becomes all the more persuasive by dint of his apparent candor and reasonableness. "Interrogators change reality," notes the Stanford psychologist Philip Zimbardo, who teaches a course in mind control. "It's not a cop—it's your Dutch uncle, your friend, the father you never had. They can change reality very quickly.". . .

Miranda and Criminal Rights

The justices who dissented from the *Miranda* opinion assumed—as did everyone else after the opinion was released on Monday, June 13, 1966—that the new *Miranda* warnings were tantamount to a ban on station-house interrogation. Everyone recognized that, from the suspect's point of view, nothing can be gained and everything can be lost by talking to the authorities without one's lawyer—and everyone assumed that the *Miranda* warnings would effectively communicate this message to most suspects.

Confession Rates Remain Unchanged

That confession rates have remained largely unchanged since *Miranda* is testimony both to psychological realities that no court could alter and to the flawed logic of the *Miranda* majority ruling. The compulsion to talk when one is accused of wrongdoing arises in part from the belief that silence is an admission of guilt. What most people do not understand, and what the *Miranda* warnings fail to explain, is that, under the Fifth Amendment, silence after arrest and *Miranda* warnings cannot be used against the defendant.

Not only are the *Miranda* warnings incomplete, they can be positively misleading in some circumstances. . . . For instance, the Supreme Court held that when police have obtained an illegal, and thus inadmissible, initial confession, they can question the suspect again without telling him that the first confession cannot be used in court. All that is needed to advise the suspect of his rights on the second interrogation, the Court said, is the standard *Miranda* warning. But the standard warning, which advises that *anything* said can be used against the suspect, implies in that situation that the first confession *can* be used against the suspect.

These are but quibbles compared to the root problem of *Miranda*: it asks police to solve crime but to protect suspects from police investigations, and it assumes that these suspects can receive adequate advice and counseling about their constitutional rights from adversaries who would like nothing more than to see those rights surrendered.

While *Miranda* has done little to change the dynamics of the interrogation process or the techniques used by police, it has affected the ex post facto analysis by courts about whether a particular confession should be admitted into evidence. *Miranda* has shifted the legal inquiry from whether the confession was voluntarily given to whether the *Miranda* rights were voluntarily waived.

A Boon to Police

There are occasional—and well-publicized—cases where the defendant has won a ruling that his confession cannot be used against him because of such a *Miranda* violation. Generally, however, the shift in focus has proven to be a boon to police. For one thing, the issue is tidier. Staccato *Miranda* conversations, with their uniform statements and check-the-box answers, are easier for courts to evaluate than sprawling hours-long interrogations. When a suspect says yes, he understands his *Miranda* rights, and yes, he waives them, he is generally taken at his word no matter how ignorant his hapless lawyer may later try to prove him. (One study of 7,000 felony cases found that defendants tried to get confessions suppressed in only 6.6 percent of the cases and succeeded in only 0.17 percent of the cases.) . . .

Confessions and Convictions

Just how important is interrogation in the arsenal of police investigative techniques? Not very, according to recent research. In the only large-scale empirical study of confessions in this country, the Institute of Criminal Law and Procedure at Georgetown University examined the results of three thousand cases in six big-city jurisdictions. The study was conducted with federal funds for the Justice Department's National Institute of Justice. Debunking the long-held assumptions of most criminal justice experts that interrogation is essential to solving crime, the study found that confessions did not guarantee that defendants would plead guilty and, further, did not increase the odds that defendants would be found guilty if they went to trial.

In half of the six jurisdictions examined, the researchers found that a confession did make it more likely that the suspect would plead guilty rather than go to trial; but in the other three jurisdictions, the opposite was found. Analyzing the results of a number of robbery and burglary cases that went to trial, the study found a high conviction rate, whether or not the suspect had confessed. In only two of the six jurisdictions (and then in only one of the two categories of cases) did a confession increase the prosecution's chances of winning by a statistically significant amount.

The researchers interviewed a number of prosecutors seeking an explanation for these surprising findings. The reason cited over and over again was the jurors' distrust of the police, particularly in the wake of any kind of police scandal no matter how unrelated to interrogation. The prosecutors also disliked confession cases because, once a confession had been obtained, there was usually little effort to gather other evidence. As one prosecutor put it: "We've been telling the cops to forget about confessions and statements. Get physical evidence. You're crazy if you even use a statement. If you have one eyewitness and a statement, you've got nothing!"

Miranda an Empty Promise

This is a typical conflict in a criminal justice system with divided goals: the police are interested in closing cases, and the prosecutors are interested in winning convictions and avoiding unnecessary controversies about defendants' rights. The Supreme Court could conclude on this evidence that the interests of the criminal justice system, not to mention the rights of the accused, would best be served by throwing out the *Miranda* apparatus and installing a simple rule of no interrogation without the presence of a neutral party or the suspect's lawyer.

That is unlikely to happen. *Miranda* has persisted this long because it allows us to celebrate our values of individualism without paying any real price. As a cultural symbol, *Miranda* stands for the enshrinement of individual rights over the need of the state for efficiency, equal justice for rich and poor before the law, the right to be presumed innocent, and the demand that the police follow the law while enforcing it. That it has managed to fail in any real sense to reform police conduct, that it serves interests opposite to those intended by its authors—this shows only that *Miranda* in twenty years has been transformed from a tool of law into an icon for our conflicting ideals.

"It is almost incontestable that the [Miranda] *decision weakened law enforcement."*

The *Miranda* Rule Has Weakened Law Enforcement

William Tucker

William Tucker, a contributor to *Harper's, The American Spectator, National Review,* and numerous other publications, is the author of *Progress and Privilege.* In the following viewpoint, Tucker argues that the *Miranda* ruling that made it mandatory for the police to inform arrested criminals of their rights undermines police officers' ability to prosecute criminals. He argues that *Miranda* obscures justice by allowing criminals to avoid confessions.

As you read, consider the following questions:

1. What statistics does the author cite to prove that *Miranda* harmed law enforcement?
2. What impact does Tucker believe *Miranda* has had on the public?
3. What impact has *Miranda* had on defense attorneys, according to the author?

When, during an appearance on *This Week with David Brinkley,* . . . Attorney General Edwin Meese used the word "infamous" to describe the *Miranda* decision—the Warren Court's ruling requiring the police to "read defendants their rights" before questioning—he generated a predictable flurry of protest. Few voices were raised in his defense, even from conservative quarters. For the principles of *Miranda,* although revolutionary, have been thoroughly, if grudgingly, incorporated into American life, accepted not only by the criminal-justice system but by most Americans.

The reason is relatively simple—the myth of the *Miranda* case is far more compelling than the reality. In the common view, *Miranda* was necessary to protect accused criminals from being forced to confess through coercion or torture. Everyone is justifiably horrified at the possibility of punishing an innocent man. In order to avoid this extreme injustice, it was argued, it might be necessary at first to let a few obviously guilty murderers, rapists, and robbers go free on "technicalities," while the police "learned the ropes." A painful price, but one most Americans eventually accepted as inevitable.

Constantly Challenged Confessions

Yet twenty years later, the police still seem to "make mistakes" all the time. Confessions are continually ruled inadmissible because they have been "coerced." Despite high-quality legal counseling—New York City has a 24-hour hotline to advise officers on constitutional issues—confessions are constantly challenged successfully in the courts. Even district attorneys are not immune to blunders. Investigations carried out under highly trained prosecutors often fail to issue in a conviction because the investigators did not "observe the defendant's constitutional rights."

Why do the police and prosecutors apparently have such trouble understanding the subtleties of *Miranda?*

The core of the problem is that the popularly accepted justification for *Miranda*—avoiding forced confessions from innocent people—had almost nothing to do with the Court's reasoning on the case. Actually, the Court was dissatisfied with the whole phenomenon of confession itself. As Chief Justice Warren wrote for the majority, the police ought to be able to solve crimes without resorting to the "cruel expedient" of forcing incriminating information out of the defendants' own mouths. . . .

The key to the presumption of innocence in our system lies in several provisions outlined in the Bill of Rights. Among them is the Fifth Amendment's guarantee that "no person . . . shall be compelled in any criminal case to be a witness against himself." Traditionally, in both England and the United States, this phrase had meant that no accused person could be compelled to take the witness stand *at his own trial*. The question that has always nagged the system, however, is this. If a person can't be forced to testify against himself at trial, why should he be forced to cooperate with the police at any point? Answering questions at the station house is, after all, just as potentially self-incriminating as answering them in court, especially when "anything you say may be held against you."

Convictions Lost

Because of [Miranda], . . . convictions are lost when police officers trip up on the technicalities, even when there is no doubt that the confession they obtain is both voluntary and reliable. . . .

Anyone who doubts that this case affected the U.S. criminal-justice system need only check the casebooks. They are filled with examples of seemingly voluntary confessions thrown out on Miranda grounds. Several years ago the California Supreme Court, relying on Miranda, reversed the conviction of a confessed triple-murderer who had been given repeated warnings of his rights and had repeatedly signed statements waiving those rights and confessing to his crime.

But the biggest cost to society of Miranda may be the statements it prevents from being made in the first place. Even those suspects eager to unburden themselves of criminal guilt may choose silence in the face of the warnings. The evidence supports the conclusion that Miranda has caused a significant drop in voluntary confessions.

Edwin Meese III, *The Wall Street Journal,* June 13, 1986.

Balanced against this are the compelling realities of police work. Like it or not, there is little the police can do, in many cases, without interrogating the suspects. With many murders, rapes, and robberies, there is little physical evidence. Eyewitness identifications, although they usually impress juries, are actually regarded as the most unreliable form of evidence by police and prosecutors. There are very few instances where an airtight case can be made from circumstantial evidence.

This does not mean that the only recourse the police have is to beat confessions out of people. Usually it is just the opposite. Guilty people often confess readily. In other cases, they offer alibis and excuses that turn out to be demonstrably false; it is only when faced with these inconsistencies and obvious falsehoods that they feel compelled to confess. . . .

While popular interpretations of *Miranda* concentrated on the image of innocent men being beaten into confessing, even the five Supreme Court Justices who made up the Warren majority on those cases were willing to admit that beatings and police brutality were not their major concern. Rather it was *confessions themselves* and the whole "coercive" atmosphere of police interrogation. Wrote Chief Justice Warren for the majority:

> To maintain a "fair state-individual balance," to require the government "to shoulder the entire load," to respect the inviolability of the human personality, our accusatory system of criminal justice demands that the government seeking to punish an individual produce the evidence against him by its own independent labors, rather than by the cruel, simple expedient of compelling it from his own mouth.

Thus, it was not simple admissions like "I did it" that the Warren majority wanted to head off. It also wanted to guard defendants against self-justifying statements and alibis that later proved to be false. The Warren majority was striking at what has long been regarded as the heart of the "detective" process.

The Criminal's Point of View

Perhaps the easiest way to summarize the Warren majority's decision is that the Justices decided to look at things from the criminal's point of view. Would a rational person ever confess to a crime? Would an individual ever open himself to certain punishment if he were surrounded by "the proper influences," as the majority wrote?

> The entire thrust of police interrogation . . . in all the cases today, was to put the defendant in such an emotional state as to impair his capacity for rational judgment. . . . The compelling atmosphere of the in-custody interrogation, and not an independent decision on his part, caused the defendant to speak.

As Justice White replied in his dissent,

> The obvious underpinning of the Court's decision is a deep-seated distrust of all confessions. . . . The result adds up to a judicial judgment that evidence from the accused should not be used against him in any way, whether compelled or not [and] that it is inherently wrong for the police to gather evidence from the accused himself.

The *Miranda* ruling addressed four cases. In none of the cases was there the slightest doubt about the individual's guilt or any reason to believe the confession had been coerced. Rather, the Court seemed to suggest the police erred by not protecting the accused sufficiently from his own poor judgment or desire to talk. . . .

One of the chief concerns of the Warren majority was that police questioning went on out of the hearing of the Court:

> Interrogation still takes place in privacy. Privacy results in

secrecy and this in turn results in a gap in our knowledge as to what in fact goes on in the interrogation rooms.

As Justice White pointed out, this was demonstrably false. Most interrogation sessions were recorded, sometimes by the detective's notes, often by a professional court stenographer. "Insofar as appears from the Court's opinion," he wrote, "it has not examined a single transcript of any police interrogation, let alone the interrogation that took place in any one of these cases which it decides today."

THE HANDCUFFS ARE ON THE WRONG MAN

Instead of trying to investigate real interrogations, however, the Warren majority undertook its most controversial tactic. It looked at several police manuals and commercial textbooks on police interrogation that were in wide circulation at the time.

The setting prescribed by the manuals and observed in practice becomes clear. In essence, it is this: To be alone with the subject is essential to prevent distraction and to deprive him of any outside support. The aura of confidence in his guilt undermines his will to resist. He merely confirms the preconceived story the police seek to have him describe. *Patience and persistence,* at times relentless questioning, are employed. To obtain a confession, the interrogator must "patiently maneuver

himself or his quarry into a position from which the desired objective may be attained."

Even without employing brutality, the "third degree" or the
specific stratagems described above, the very fact of custodial
interrogation exacts a heavy toll on individual liberty and trades
on the weakness of individuals. . . . [My emphasis.]

Some of the tactics described in the interrogation manuals were
admittedly manipulative and would easily be acknowledged as
illegal today. But for the most part, the manuals recommend only
what the Warren majority referred to—critically—as "patience and
persistence." The books outline the "good cop, bad cop" routine,
where one officer tries to win the defendant's confidence, while
the other questions him harshly. One manual even recommends
that, if the suspect exercises his right to remain silent, the request
should be readily granted. "This usually has a very undermining
effect. First of all, he is disappointed in his expectation of an unfavorable reaction on the part of the interrogator. Secondly, a con-
cession of this right to remain silent impresses the subject with
the apparent fairness of the interrogator." For the most part, the
investigative techniques to which the Warren Court objected do
no more than take advantage of a common-sense grasp of human
psychology. . . .

Miranda Weakened Law Enforcement

Now, twenty years after *Miranda*, it is almost incontestable that
the decision weakened law enforcement, especially during the late
1960s and early 1970s. It is also very likely that it contributed to
the surge in crime rates during that period.

In the years following *Miranda*, convictions won through trials
stayed at a remarkably stable 10 to 12 per cent. That might lead
to the belief that *Miranda* had changed nothing. The real action,
however, was among the 90 per cent of cases that are settled by
plea-bargaining. There *Miranda* changed everything.

Before *Miranda*, when police had reached a stage where they
were fairly certain they had solved a crime, they sought a confession to make the case airtight. Now it was not so easy, and even
if the confession was obtained, it might be thrown out of court
as "coerced." Somewhat less sure that they could make their cases
invincible, prosecutors were more willing to bargain and regularly
gave ground. And then, because motions and appeals to *Miranda*
and other Warren decisions were clogging the courts, prosecutors
became even more willing to deal. . . .

In 1966, more than 60 per cent of accused persons pleaded guilty
to the *original* charges, while 27 per cent of the cases were resolved
by guilty pleas to *reduced* charges. One year later the entire pattern had changed remarkably. In 1967 alone, pleas on the original
charges dropped to 42 per cent, while reduced pleas rose to 39
per cent. The change was never as dramatic after 1967, but the

drift was inexorable. By 1973, 47 per cent of all cases were settled on *reduced* charges (up from 29 per cent) while only 39 per cent were pleaded at the original top charge (down from 60 per cent). In the same year, out of 31,000 felony arrests made in Manhattan, only 4,100 resulted in *felony* convictions. The vast majority were plea-bargained down to misdemeanors.

Criminals Released

Nearly as important as *Miranda*'s effects on police and prosecutors were its effects on the public, which was severely demoralized by seeing confessed criminals go free on "improper warnings" in a number of highly visible cases. In Philadelphia one murderer was let off because the *"Miranda* card" used in that city read, "anything you say may be held *for or* against you," thus, according to the courts, "creating a false sense of security." In another case a murderer confessed to a friend, an ex-con turned police informer, and the confession was excluded on the grounds that the informer, as a police agent, should have read the murderer his rights. The courts have allowed utterly voluntary confessions, offered by criminals with tormented consciences, to be withdrawn later on the grounds that what was voluntarily given could be voluntarily withdrawn. Not infrequently, criminals who, after consultation with counsel, nevertheless decided to confess have had their confessions thrown out subsequently on the grounds that their lawyers must have been incompetent to have allowed them to confess in the first place. In some states it almost seems as if it is *illegal* to confess.

There can be no doubt as to the effect of all this. There is nothing more horrifying to the average person than the sense that the state cannot even deal with *confessed* criminals. It is hugely demoralizing. People become afraid to stand up to crime because they fear the government is weak or not on their side. This paralyzing fear that "the criminals are winning" then becomes itself a major impediment to law enforcement. . . .

Criminals Continue To Confess

The Warren Court's efforts to "look at things from the criminal's point of view" (as the majority specifically stated in one of the *Miranda* cases) has had a profound impact on American life. Perhaps the strangest outcome of all, however, is that, despite all the procedural safeguards that the Warren Court put in place, *criminals still regularly confess to crimes.* . . .

To be sure, many confessed criminals decide *afterward* that maybe they would have been smarter to keep their mouths shut. But that is a different story altogether.

Every police detective I have interviewed has made the same observation. Quite contrary to the Warren Court's implicit assumption that confession is so irrational that it can only be explained by some sort of coercion, police experts say that, in one way or another, most criminals *want to confess*. . . .

Criminals want to confess, but they want their confessions to be "off the record." They want the psychological relief and purging that come with admitting their role in something, but they don't necessarily want to live with the consequences.

It is at this moment that the defense attorney enters. One way or another, he argues, the confession was "involuntarily, unknowingly, and unwillingly given." Why, he asks incredulously, would anyone admit to such a thing when he knew his statement would be self-incriminating?

After Reality Sets In

Six months later, the trial judge encounters a neatly dressed, polite, composed defendant who tells him sincerely that his incriminating statements were coerced from him by the police. Three years later, five appellate-court judges will look at the written record of the trial and say to each other, "Why would anyone ever admit to all this stuff? The police must have coerced him. He never would have said these things on his own."

And so, the prosecution will be forced to go back and retry the defendant "without the confession"—*and without any other evidence that was produced as a result of the confession.* For nothing gathered as the *result* of a confession is admissible evidence once the confession is ruled unconstitutional. . . .

Even few *confessed* criminals, then, are willing to stand by their confession very long. Once they have purged themselves of guilt feelings, or rationalized their crimes, reality sets in. At the very least, their lawyers will coach them to come up with a different story, and will routinely challenge the constitutionality of their confession.

All this, however, does not mean that people are not guilty, or that they don't confess to crimes. All it means is that after they have confessed, they have a body of law to help them repudiate their confessions. *Miranda*'s largest impact, in the end, has not been on defendants but on defense lawyers. They routinely arrive on the scene and charge that the police have already coerced their new clients into confessing.

But beneath these legal manipulations lies the truth. Trials were once forums in which society tried to find out what really happened. If they no longer function that way, then we must live without knowing the truth. But somehow the truth has a way of emerging anyway.

Distinguishing Bias from Reason

Many people have strong feelings about what rights those accused of crime should have. When dealing with controversial issues, often people respond based on their emotions rather than on their powers of reason. Thus, one of the most important basic thinking skills is the ability to distinguish between statements based upon emotions and those based on a consideration of facts.

Most of the following statements are taken from the viewpoints in this chapter. Consider each statement carefully. *Mark R for any statement you believe is based on reason and a rational consideration of the facts. Mark B for any statement you believe is based on bias, prejudice, or emotion. Mark I for any statement you think is impossible to judge.*

If you are doing this exercise as a member of a class or group, compare your answers with those of other class or group members. Be able to defend your answers. You may discover that others will come to different conclusions than you. Listening to the reasons others present for their answers may give you valuable insights in distinguishing between bias and reason.

If you are reading this book alone, ask others if they agree with your answers. You will find this interaction valuable also.

R = *a statement based upon reason*
B = *a statement based upon bias*
I = *a statement impossible to judge*

130

1. Crime in the U.S. is rampant. New York City has 20 times as many murders as the country of Sweden even though their populations are about the same.

2. Hardened criminals who commit heinous crimes do not deserve clever lawyers who will help them get off scot-free.

3. Studies have found that *Miranda* warnings have little or no effect on a suspect's likelihood to talk.

4. When released 20 years ago, the *Miranda* decision quickly became the most reviled decision ever issued by the Supreme Court.

5. The principles of *Miranda* have been thoroughly incorporated into American life and accepted by the criminal justice system and most Americans.

6. The rights of defendants have never been a popular cause.

7. The poor are at a disadvantage at every point in the proceedings of the criminal justice system.

8. Most poor people accused of crime are appointed public defenders who do not spend much time on the case. The average time in court per case for a public defender was only 1.7 hours.

9. Everyone is justifiably horrified at the possibility of punishing an innocent man.

10. After being a judge for 10 years I've seen that most guilty pleas are still entered by poor, ignorant, frightened people who do not understand their rights.

11. Now, 20 years after *Miranda,* it is almost incontestable that the decision weakened law enforcement.

12. *Miranda* led to more plea bargaining. Out of 31,000 felony arrests made in Manhattan, only 4,100 resulted in felony convictions. Most were plea bargained down to misdemeanors.

13. The man who mugged me and held a knife to my throat should not have been set free because the police officer forgot to read him his *Miranda* rights.

14. Experts now agree that no positive identification of a suspect can be made based on a few hairs found at the scene of the crime.

15. Deterrence is the primary core of any effective response to the reign of terror in American cities.

16. The interests of the criminal justice system would be best served by throwing out *Miranda* and installing a simple rule of no questioning without the suspect's lawyer.

Periodical Bibliography

The following list of periodical articles deals with the subject matter of this chapter.

Warren T. Brookes — "Crime, the Jobless and a Bad Theory," *The Washington Times*, August 29, 1985.

Gerald M. Caplan — "Questioning *Miranda*," *Vanderbilt Law Review*, November 1985.

Adam Dershowitz — "Even Bad People Have Rights," *The Washington Times*, March 21, 1985.

Robert Jacobs — "The State of *Miranda*," *Trial*, January 1985.

Yale Kamisar — "The *Miranda* Case, 20 Years Later," *The New York Times*, June 11, 1986.

Edward I. Koch — "Crime and Poverty," *USA Today*, March 1985.

John Leo — "Are Criminals Born, Not Made?" *Time*, October 21, 1985.

Ira A. Lipman — "The Economic Power of Crime," *Vital Speeches of the Day*, August 1, 1984.

Herbert I. London — "Stating the Obvious About Crime," *USA Today*, November 1984.

Thomas Main — "Is There a Bias in Favor of the Guilty?" *The Washington Times*, October 29, 1985.

Edwin Meese III — "Square *Miranda* Rights with Reason," *The Wall Street Journal*, June 13, 1986.

Notre Dame Law Review — "The Compelled Confession: A Case Against Admissibility," 1985.

Nicholas Pileggi — "Meet the Muggers," *New York*, March 9, 1981.

Reader's Digest — "Crime and Punishment USA," December 1985.

W.S. White — "Defending *Miranda*: A Reply to Professor Caplan," *Vanderbilt Law Review*, January 1986.

Wisconsin Law Review — "Corroborating Confessions: Legal Safeguards Against False Confessions," 1984.

Michael Zander — "Suspects' Rights: An Irony," *The New York Times*, January 27, 1986.

Should the Criminal Justice System Enforce Crime Victims' Rights?

CRIMINAL JUSTICE

"A growing body of evidence indicates that disregard for the rights of victims . . . has placed serious psychological burdens on crime victims."

Crime Victims Need More Legal Rights

Judith Miller and Mark Miller

Judith Miller and Mark Miller are investigative reporters whose work has appeared in many national magazines. In the following viewpoint, the authors cite new laws that allow victims more involvement in the criminal justice system. They argue that the victim has too often been ignored and that these new laws improve the system considerably.

As you read, consider the following questions:

1. What was Betty Spencer's impression of the criminal justice system? Why?
2. How are crime victims affected by their experience, according to the authors?
3. How, according to the authors, do new laws help crime victims recover?

Judith Miller and Mark Miller, "Where Are Our Rights?" Reprinted from USA TODAY Magazine, May 1986. Copyright by the Society for the Advancement of Education.

"Many victims are soon forgotten," says Betty Jane Spencer. "Many cannot speak out to let the public know how they feel. There are those who are suffering so from their traumatic experience that they silently wait for someone to help them, but help has been slow in coming. There are those who cannot speak out because they are dead. I feel sure that all victims are asking the same question! Where are *my* rights?"

Sometime after midnight on Feb. 14, 1977, four youths, armed with shotguns, broke into the Spencer's rural Indiana home. First, they robbed them, tearing the place apart, then they ordered Spencer and her four young sons, ranging in age from 14 to 22, to lie side by side on the floor. They shot all five of them. Betty Jane Spencer survived three shotgun blasts, but her four sons were killed.

Three weeks later, the first of the four killers was caught. He confessed to the murders and named the other three. In his confession, he said that his gang had wanted to see what it was like to kill someone—that they had plotted to pick out a house at random and kill everyone in that house just for the fun of it, for something to do.

The confession of the second killer caught was almost a duplicate of the first youth's confession. However, shortly thereafter, Spencer was shocked to learn, after confessing to the murders of her sons, the two killers suddenly pleaded not guilty. When she asked the County Prosecutor about this development, he told her that this was their legal right.

Victim Ignored

Spencer was outraged because, she felt, her rights as well as her boys' rights had been violated. Her impression of the judicial process was that her dead sons had no rights, while the killers' rights were being carefully protected. The four killers, for example, were free to discuss the case with anyone, yet she was told to only talk about what had happened with the Prosecutor or the Indiana State Police, because she could have said something to jeopardize one of the trials had she talked about the case. The further they got into preparations for the trials, the more confused she became.

"The State paid for both the defense and the prosecution of these four, but my husband and I had to find a way to pay the $22,000 this crime cost us," says Spencer. "About $10,000 was covered by insurance, the other $12,000 was our problem. Indiana did not have victims' compensation at that time." Her words have been repeated by many other victims of violent crime who, after suf-

135

BERRY'S WORLD By Jim Berry

"OK — now that the criminal is back on the streets, you victims are free to go."

fering brutal attacks, turned to their government for help, only to receive little or none.

In 1984 alone, 6,000,000 people were victims of violent crime. Half of these victims didn't bother to report the attack because they felt the system wasn't designed to protect their rights. The other 3,000,000, who courageously came forward, were frequently trapped in a web of lengthy, frustrating court trials and left with deep psychological scars. According to a Nov. 30, 1984 report by the American Psychological Association (APA) Task Force on the

Victims of Crime and Violence, "Billions have been spent to apprehend, prosecute, incarcerate, rehabilitate, and study criminals, but almost nothing to compensate, rehabilitate, and study victims."

Psychological Scars

A growing body of evidence indicates that disregard for the rights of victims as a matter of public and legal policy has placed serious psychological burdens on crime victims. Having endured an unprovoked attack, victims are then doubly victimized when they discover that the primary concern of public authorities, as expressed through our criminal justice system, is to arrest, prosecute, sentence, and incarcerate the criminal. In their quest to accomplish this task, the system's funds go almost entirely to law enforcement and to protect the rights of the criminal, while little is left over to help the hapless victim. According to the APA report:

> Even when the criminal is apprehended and prosecuted, the victim quickly learns that the prosecutor represents all the people and not the individual victim. Having experienced loss at the criminal's hands, the victim now experiences a loss of identity as well. It is clear that countless injustices suffered during the criminal process seriously complicated the victim's psychological adaptation.

Dr. Shelley Neiderbach, for example, five years after she had been attacked and pistol-whipped in her car in Brooklyn, was mugged at knifepoint in her apartment building lobby. She recognized the mugger as a member of a neighborhood juvenile gang. However, she was afraid to testify against him for fear of retaliation. "When a psychopath puts a gun to your head or a knife to your throat, it's a life-changing, life-shattering piece of evil," Neiderbach told reporters March 5, 1985. "I didn't know what to do. I felt vulnerable, helpless, powerless, rage. I had to do something."

Victims show immediate emotional reactions to the traumatizing attack. These are followed in a few days by other short-term emotional reactions and changes in behavior. Some behavioral reactions linger and endure into long-term reactions that can be very painful. For example, anger, shock, disbelief, confusion, fear, and anxiety are reported by investigators to be some of the immediate reactions of rape victims. Yet, when a 13-year-old girl was beaten and raped in the back of a car in Pittsburgh, the court was far from compassionate. The county judge, J. Quint Salmon, dismissed the rape charge because the girl who had filed the complaint was late to court. Only after protestors picketed at the county courthouse and at the home of the judge in March, 1985 in reaction to this dismissal did Salmon reinstate the rape charge.

Rape, robbery, and assault victims tend to perceive themselves as helpless, weak, frightened, or out of control immediately after the attack. Sleep disturbances, nightmares, diarrhea, headaches, an increase in psychosomatic symptoms, and an aggravation of any prior health problems also are among the immediate reactions.

After a few days, the victims' symptoms can include anger, fear, anxiety, tension, humiliation, embarrassment, revenge, and self-blame. Loss of identity and self-respect may follow victimization. When victims are physically injured, they experience not only rage, but also grief and depression over the loss of normal functioning. In fact, the APA notes, "severe depression is common in rape victims."

Sometimes, victims reexperience the traumatic event in the form of obsessions or recurrent dreams and nightmares, and often show decreased interest in social and sexual relations. One 40-year-old woman who had been raped by a boarder in her home when she was four years old was haunted throughout her life by this awful memory. After 36 years, she finally sought psychiatric treatment and, under hypnosis, relived this attack from her childhood. The psychiatric treatment helped her recover her feelings of power as a person that she felt she had been robbed of years before. . . .

New Laws Help Victims

For too long, victims of crime have been at the mercy of an indifferent government. However, a new awareness by society of their suffering has recently brought important changes and hope for the future. For example, after Neiderbach was attacked the second time, she decided to do something. What she did was to devote herself to counseling other crime victims in New York City, founding a free service that includes several psychologists.

Compassion for Victims

To have a responsible view on criminal justice issues, in the view of this observer, it is not necessary that you be for or against the death penalty. It is necessary, however, that you have *at least as much* compassion for the needs of the innocent and of society as a whole as you have for the defendants and for the criminals.

Patrick B. McGuigan, *Conservative Digest,* March 1984.

New York has enacted new laws to protect the rights of victims. Crime victims will get more money from New York under a law signed by Gov. Mario Cuomo in August, 1985. The law uses $6,500,000 in Federal funds to allow the State Crime Victims Board to increase aid.

In March, 1985, New York passed a law that gives a victim the chance to present a statement to the judge before the criminal is sentenced. "Before this, we have always concerned ourselves with pre-sentence information concerning the defendant," State Sen.

Ralph Marino, a sponsor of the measure, told the press when the law was passed. "The victim has had very little consideration in the criminal-justice system. Now we're getting to victims' rights, for a change. The victim, for the first time, really has access to the judge's ear—whether there should be restitution and how much, what the jail sentence should be." Too frequently, judges never see the victim or hear the victim's side of the story before sentencing a convicted attacker. This law permits judges to listen to the victim's story and thus hear the victim's views.

The Victim's Viewpoint

Victims can provide a judge with valuable information, helping to ensure that a fair sentence can be provided. Under this law, every pre-sentence report done for a convicted criminal must contain a "victim's impact statement," which will include an analysis of the victim's version of the crime, a description of the extent of injury to the victim and/or the victim's property, and the victim's viewpoint concerning an appropriate sentence for the suffering that was inflicted by the criminal. In the case of homicide, the victim's family will be permitted to submit a statement. However, victims or their families are not required to give a statement against their wishes.

Clearly, as much must be done to safeguard the rights of victims as that done to protect the rights of criminals. Consider this travesty of justice: A man was convicted in 1974 of sexually assaulting a child. He repeated the offense and, in 1980, was convicted again and sentenced to 18 months. He served seven months. After that, he was arrested again for molesting a seven-year-old, released on bail, and, while out on bail, molested yet another child. Our criminal justice system was apparently doing all it could for the rights of the child molester, but where was it for those four helpless children whom that man molested? *Where were their rights?*

"When we let the victim's personal feelings affect the judge's sentence we are reverting to a government not of laws, but of men."

Victims' Legal Rights May Undermine Justice

Hiller B. Zobel

Hiller B. Zobel is an associate justice of the Massachusetts Superior Court. In the following viewpoint, Zobel argues that victims' involvement in the court system has its negative side. Victims' testimony in court is necessarily highly emotional and evokes sympathy from the judge, he writes, but in the end courts must still be fair to the criminal. Judges should not make decisions based on emotion, but rather by careful consideration of the facts in the case.

As you read, consider the following questions:

1. What point does the author make with his example of the rape case trial?
2. How is the criminal justice system concept of equal treatment under the law harmed by victim participation, according to the author?
3. Why does Zobel believe retribution is bad?

Hiller B. Zobel, "Victims' Rights," *The Christian Science Monitor*, January 16, 1985. Copyright © 1985, Hiller B. Zobel. Reprinted with the author's permission.

At the trial of aggravated rape, although the 17-year-old swore the two young men had raped her at the party, they said she had consented to everything. After deliberating almost three days, the jury could not decide.

When the retrial began before a different judge, the prosecutor agreed that if the defendants would plead guilty, he would reduce the charge to ordinary rape and would recommend an easy sentence.

His reasoning was simple. If the evidence could not persuade one jury, perhaps it would leave the second equally uncertain. Indeed, one or both defendants might achieve acquittal. And regardless of the outcome, the teen-ager would have to go through the embarrassment of testifying and the ordeal of cross-examination.

The defendants reasoned similarly, but to an opposite conclusion, and with no concern for the youngster. Better to admit guilt of the lesser offense than chance conviction on the more serious charge.

Victim Addresses the Court

When the men came up for sentencing, the teenager asked to address the court, a right a recently enacted statute had given all victims of crime.

Accompanied by her parents, she came before the bench and in an emotional appeal, asked for severe punishment. This was quite understandable and usual, even though the problems of the case had induced the prosecutor to suggest light punishment.

This time, however, the parents added their own imprecations. The judge, himself a parent, understood their vehemence but found it disturbing.

Because, under all circumstances, the recommended sentence was entirely appropriate, the judge imposed it. Yet he remained puzzled. He knew that the evidence in the case raised serious questions as to the degree of parental supervision involved. Were the parents, he wondered, acting out some of their own feelings?

Sometime later, entirely by chance, the judge learned that one of the vociferously vengeful parents was, at the time the sentence was passing, a probationer of that same court.

Victims' Rights Need Rethinking

The whole concept of "victims' rights" needs careful rethinking. It is deceptively easy to insist that a person who has been subjected to the depredations of a criminal should receive from judges no less consideration than the criminal himself gets. As one who has himself been heldup at gunpoint and taken across the state, I can readily endorse that idea.

Problems arise, however, when we try to fit the equal-treatment precept into a judicial system that wisely refuses to consider anyone a criminal unless and until a jury decides that the government has—beyond a reasonable doubt—proved him one. The inescapable consequence of this fundamental principle is that up to verdict (or until the defendant pleads guilty), the person who seems to be a "victim" is only a "complaining witness."

Diminishing Accuseds' Rights

"Victim" and "accused" are labels. Both deserve to be treated fairly. Yet the result of our increased concern for victims has actually diminished the rights of the accused more than it has protected the rights of victims.

John J. Cleary, *USA Today*, April 19, 1984.

But, you say, what about after verdict or plea? Surely then we can drop the quotation marks and start paying some real attention to the victim.

A Wild Kind of Justice

Even here, we face difficulties. First, many victims—particularly victims of personal violence—want retribution. That is only natural. But as Bacon said centuries ago, "Revenge is a kind of wild justice; which the more man's nature runs to, the more ought law to weed it out." When we let the victim's personal feelings affect the judge's sentence we are reverting to a government not of laws, but of men.

Beyond that, a victim rarely makes his statement to the judge under oath; and never subject to cross-examination. The victim's input comes to the judge completely untested. He is shown only one aspect of what is almost always an extremely complex matter.

That is why, when a victim (or someone close to a victim) addresses the court, a judge always listens sympathetically, but proceeds most cautiously.

3

"The criminal justice system must become a haven for those victimized by those who violate the law."

Victims' Rights Laws Protect the Victim

John Heinz

Within the last ten years, many laws have been passed to protect victims' rights at both the state and federal level. Some of these laws require victim participation in criminal hearings, restitution by the criminal, mandatory pretrial detention, and other restraints on the criminal. In the following viewpoint, John Heinz argues that these laws vastly improve the plight of the victim. He believes the criminal justice system is finally standing up for the rights of victims rather than earnestly protecting the guilty criminal. Heinz is a Republican senator and chair of the Special Committee on Aging, which serves in an ombudsman role for all federal issues affecting the nation's elderly.

As you read, consider the following questions:

1. Why does the author applaud recent federal legislation to protect the victim?
2. How do stringent victims' rights laws increase crime reports by victims, according to Heinz?

John Heinz, "Recognizing the Rights of Crime Victims." Reprinted from USA TODAY Magazine, July 1984. Copyright by the Society for the Advancement of Education.

The national crime clock is ticking. Every 24 seconds nationwide, a violent crime occurs. Every 23 minutes, that violence is murder; every six seconds, a woman is being raped; every eight seconds, a home is burglarized; every 29 seconds, a car or truck is vandalized by thieves.

Dollar figures also tell the tale of crime. Robberies cost the American public an average of $355,000 every day. Arson destroys an estimated $3,500,000 in property per day. White-collar crime sucks $110,000,000 a day from our ailing economy. Store burglaries—from "mom and pop" stores to large department stores—rack up $83,000,000,000 in losses to American business annually. Moreover, we all pay a crime excise tax on purchased goods—to cover the projected costs of expected losses as well as the known costs of hired protection to keep those losses to a minimum.

For Every Crime

However measured, statistics gloss over one of the most troublesome consequences of crime in America today. For every crime counted, there are innocent victims: those directly assaulted, those whose homes and businesses are entered and rifled, as well as the families, neighbors, and loved ones who share in the victims' pain and loss or who must cope with their own losses as survivors. That law-and-order process designed to apprehend those who break the law, to enforce our penal code against those who would evade it, and to lead the victimized through the judiciary's procedural maze falls down on the job with that final assignment. These individuals—the victims of robberies or assaults, the families who are victimized by a loved one's murder, the businessperson whose enterprise has been victimized by vandals or employees—become ciphers in a game the sole purpose of which is closing the case. Emotional trauma, social stigma, tangible losses or physical injury go unattended to by police, prosecutors, and all strata of criminal justice officials. An ability to separate a victim's personal well-being from his or her victimization appears to be a job criteria for criminal justice officials. The old TV star, Sergeant Joe Friday of "Dragnet," played the role adeptly with his automatic line, "Just the facts, ma'am." . . .

How can we urge individuals to come forward and participate in a criminal justice process which recognizes the rights of only the accused? New York State officials assert that 90% of all crimes which are eventually solved rely upon the voluntary participation of a victim or a witness. Yet, national victimization surveys

144

repeatedly show that half of all crimes are never even reported to the police; and, for every 10 persons who do report the crime and begin the steps toward prosecution, four of them drop out. Meanwhile, district attorneys across the country cite the low levels of victim participation as the prime reason for a low percentage of prosecutions.

Stereotyping Victims

Our stereotypical concept of a crime victim is the elderly woman whose purse is snatched by the quick thief or the homeowner who arrives home to find his or her house dismantled and stripped of all its valuable possessions. However, that population is much broader; the impact of a victimization ripples its way through many interconnected lives. The divorce rate among married rape victims—divorces which occur within six months of the attack—is nearly 50% due to the psychological trauma inflicted on both equally innocent partners. . . .

Victim Laws Are Just

Victims'-rights advocates . . . work within the system, making it fairer for victims—and for the public at large. Twenty states now allow victims to submit a written "impact statement" detailing the injuries or damages suffered as a result of the crime. In another half-dozen states, the victim may offer opinions concerning what sentence is appropriate. Four states—Arizona, California, Connecticut and New Hampshire—go a step further and permit the victims to present evidence and express opinions in person or through counsel. In addition, many special "Victims Assistance Units" have been set up across the country to make sure that victims' concerns are met. . . .

It would not be surprising to see the efforts of the victims' movement crowned with increasing success. After all, if you ignore the victims of crime in a democracy long enough, there will soon be too many of them.

William Tucker, *Reader's Digest*, June 1985.

Obviously, the list of problems and the exposition of shocking, heartrending examples is lengthy. The question at hand is two-fold: what *is* being done on behalf of victims and witnesses of crime, and what more *can* be done? During the past decade, the U.S. Department of Justice spent over $50,000,000 on victim and witness assistance projects nationwide. That seed money, no longer available, left behind numerous programs, many of which have survived, even in the present era of austerity. These include a mixture of victim/witness assistance units in prosecutors' offices and police departments, rape crisis centers, child abuse and domestic violence shelters, and programs for elderly victims. It is estimated, however, that less than five per cent of all law enforcement agencies nationwide have services available where they can refer victims needing emergency aid. Similarly, less than 10% of all prosecutors' offices nationwide have established programs to aid victims.

Where services are offered, it is important to recognize that results can be seen. Take, for example, the rape care center—recently expanded to aid victims of other violent crimes as well—in Des Moines, Iowa. Prior to the center's existence, only one-third of Polk County's rape cases resulted in charges being filed against an accused assailant. That rate has now more than doubled to 75%, the conviction rate also has doubled, moving from 40% to 80%.

Long-Term, Comprehensive Aid Needed

Note that such programs are, by definition and necessity, crisis-oriented. Because of limited budgets, their emphasis is rarely on long-term counseling. Thus, while these voluntary community-based support groups can be critical, they can not provide the broad-based victim and witness assistance which is generally recognized to be seriously deficient. The model of "peer counseling" of families bereaved after a murder is a new variant of victims assistance which points the way to a new service provider method. Another concern among crisis intervention aides is that their well-intentioned help can, at times, do more harm than good. Asking the "wrong" question—a simple "why did you leave the back door unlocked?"—which is intended to elicit information, can backfire when interpreted as an accusatory jab. Thus, the crisis intervention specialists in the field are themselves looking for more advisory help from mental health professionals and resources to offer extensive, standardized training for both staff and volunteers. . . .

Holes in the Safety Net

This progress is promising and encouraging—and also somewhat misleading. The leaders of national victims' rights organizations are quick to point out the holes in the statewide victim safety net; some states have not appropriated adequate funding for their victims' compensation plans, so that valid claims often go unpaid for long periods of time. Georgia, for instance, has a "Good Samaritan Act" (the popular term for statutes protecting individuals who seek to prevent a crime or apprehend a criminal, thereby incurring personal injury or damage), which helps only those injured while assisting another individual or a police officer during a crime in progress. Many local programs have suffered during these tough economic times, curtailing services or actually closing doors. So, the picture in general is one of two steps forward, one—or sometimes two—steps back.

146

We have, however, achieved a major victory at the Federal level. On. Oct. 12, [1982] the President signed into law the 1982 Victims and Witness Protection Act, legislation which Sen. Paul Laxalt (R.-Nev.) and I introduced in April, 1982. This is the first piece of victims' rights legislation ever to pass the Congress, and the first substantial anti-crime measure to be signed into law in four years. This new law not only intercedes on behalf of victims of all nature of Federal crimes, it will serve as a model and a prod to those states which have yet to recognize the rights of crime victims in a constructive fashion. This is a package of do-able, no cost, administrative and procedural reforms which will have an immediate and palpable effect on the way victims of crime are treated by those who represent our Federal legal system. With these guidelines and remedies in hand, no longer will the victims of Federal crimes need to think twice about coming forward as active participants in the pursuit and conviction of those who have violated the individual and legal rights of others.

The final version of the Heinz-Laxalt bill, agreed to by all 535 Members of Congress, breaks new ground in the following areas. It institutes the use of Victim Impact Statements, so that judges

Steve Kelley for the *San Diego Union*. Reprinted with permission.

hearing Federal cases will be apprised prior to sentencing an offender of the harm caused—the physical, financial, and emotional
injuries inflicted on the crime's victims. Sentencing by the book
without regard for the individual human toll taken is a malad-
ministration of justice. Restitution—currently an option rarely ex-
ercised by judges—will be made a requirement of the sentence
whenever monetary losses, whether they be for medical bills or
replacement of stolen or damaged property, have been incurred
by the victim. In the event the judge reasons restitution is unnecessary, that reasoning is required to become part of the
record. . . .

The new law will expand the Attorney General's powers to protect both victims and witnesses from the intimidation and har-
rassment which all too often go hand in hand with any agreement
to assist and cooperate with the prosecutorial system. Bringing
the accused to his or her day in court should never be
accomplished at a risk to those victims who are seeking punishment for their assailants. Perhaps the most far-reaching statutory
language in the new law is that which establishes guidelines for
the fair treatment of victims and witnesses. These "little things"
are those which, to me, create the cruelest mockery of criminal
justice; the new guidelines seek to correct these patterns of
bureaucratic abuse and neglect of victims and witnesses. . . .

Victims Are People

The Victim and Witness Protection Act will make it mandatory
to inform the victim of the case's progress, whether that information relates to the police investigation, a change in hearing date
or location, or a release of the accused on bail or the offender from
prison. It will require consultations with the victim before enter-
ing into a plea bargain or dismissing a case. The new guidelines
will make the prompt return of recovered personal property the
rule, not the exception, and remind criminal justice officials that
photographs of personal goods will indeed suffice for evidentiary
purposes. These new fair treatment guidelines will statutorily remind criminal justice officials that victims, too, are people. . . .

Another proposal I shall continue to work into legislative form
would set up a Federal victims' compensation fund, into which
would be deposited fines levied against all persons convicted of
their crimes. Obviously, such a system could not afford 100% compensation for all crime victims, but it could provide at least par-
tial recoupment of financial losses suffered by the victims of such
strictly Federal crimes as airline hijackings. . . .

The Limits of Restitution

An important caveat needs to be flagged at this point.
Restitution—while a vital victims service—will touch only a small
portion of this population. Since less than 20% of all crimes lead

to an arrest, less than 10% of the accused are ever prosecuted, and less than three per cent of those arrested are actually convicted, 97% of all victims would go unaided if restitution were their only means of assistance or retribution. Therefore, while financial losses are indeed most often devastating, the rights of victims must be represented at every stage of the process, not just in the final pay-out, if it is ever reached. Moreover, if the process itself is not made more humanitarian, the participation rate among victims and witnesses will continue to plod at low levels, keeping the conviction rate at a depressingly retarded one, a prospect this nation must not perpetuate. . . .

Standing Up for the Victim

The criminal justice system can stand up for the rights of the innocent victim, rather than blindly and unilaterally protecting the rights of the innocent-until-proven-guilty criminal. The criminal justice system must become a haven for those victimized by those who violate the law, rather than just for those who seek the constitutional protections afforded them in spite of their criminal activity. Those who have dubbed the process the "criminal injustice system" must have new cause to believe in its righteous pursuit of justice fully respective of the needs of innocent victims.

We must all begin listening to the overly large population of victims when they tell us, as our committee was told by a kidnapping victim, "Don't confuse cold with professional. We need to examine our own feelings about crime. Because of our discomfort with the issue of crime, society tends to treat its victims as anathema. Ask them to emphasize respect."

This new law instills this respect in the process itself. While it is distressing that the justice system's sensitivity toward people requires statutory definition, Congress has now leaped the first hurdle on behalf of victims. Society must help us carry the ball to keep others from being victimized both by those who choose to break the law and by those who are charged with enforcing it.

4

"[Victims' rights] has come to mean some undefined, yet irreducible right of crime victims that 'trumps' the rights of criminal defendants."

Victims' Rights Laws Exploit the Victim

Lynne N. Henderson

Lynne N. Henderson is an assistant professor of law at Florida State University. In the following viewpoint, Henderson argues that new laws that ostensibly protect victims' rights are merely a way to enforce conservative methods of crime control. By placing an emphasis on victim participation at the end of the process—such as sentencing, restitution, and trial, she argues, victims' needs are bypassed. If victims' needs were truly considered by the criminal justice system, psychological treatment would be available to help victims recover from crime. New laws emphasizing retribution and vengeance cannot help victims, she believes.

As you read, consider the following questions:

1. Why does the author believe that current victims' rights trends undermine victims' psychological recovery?
2. Does the author believe that the criminal justice system "revictimizes the victim"? Why or why not?
3. Why does Henderson argue that the criminal does not really have any advantage over the victim in the criminal justice system?

Lynne N. Henderson, "The Wrongs of Victim's Rights," *Stanford Law Review,* Volume 37, page 937, April 1985. Copyright 1985 by the Board of Trustees of the Leland Stanford Junior University.

The issue of "rights" for victims of crime has become influential in shaping criminal law and procedure. In 1982 alone, California voters approved a "Victim's Bill of Rights" that made substantial changes in California law, and the President's Task Force on Victims of Crime issued its final report, recommending numerous changes in the criminal justice system. The influence of the victim's rights "movement" appears to be creating a new era in American criminal law and procedure. . . .

Using the Victim's Image

While law enforcement officers and prosecutors have long understood the symbolic value of the victim, the politicization of the symbol is of more recent origin. The complaint of officers and prosecutors that the courts "never think about the victim" when deciding cases in favor of defendants made "intuitive" sense: A violent crime involves at least two persons, but the focus seemed to be only on the one least "deserving" of attention or regard—the offender. Although for quite some time this argument had been only sporadically raised, by the middle of the 1970s different groups began to focus their attention on the victims of particular crimes. For example, the women's movement did much to emphasize the plight of rape victims in the legal process, while the more recently formed group, "Mothers Against Drunk Driving" (hereinafter referred to as MADD), brought the victims of drunk drivers to public attention. The success of these groups concerned with particular crimes and crime victims served to highlight the general importance of "victims" as an effective political symbol. Conservatives thus began rhetorically to paint "the victim" as a sympathetic figure whose rights and interests could be used to counterbalance the defendant's rights, and called for a new balance to be struck by courts and legislatures.

As a result of the convergence of these factors, the subject of "victim's rights" has received enormous political, media, and legal attention. Both Congress and the states have enacted victim's rights legislation, the President's Task Force on Victims of Crime has published its final report, and groups such as MADD and "Parents of Murdered Children" continue to receive national attention. Victim's rights proponents have succeeded in inducing the adoption of preventive detention laws in at least nine states. Victim's rights advocates have played a role in bringing about other changes in criminal law and procedure. Partly as a result of victim's rights advocacy, the number of laws requiring mandatory restitution to victims by offenders has also increased. . . .

151

Most of the victim's rights activity has been far from dispassionate, and currently, the victim's rights "movement" has a decidedly conservative bent. Although "victim's rights" may be viewed as a populist movement responding to perceived injustices in the criminal process, genuine questions about victims and victimization have become increasingly coopted by the concerns of advocates of the "crime control" model of criminal justice.

A Blameless Stereotype

The phrase "victim's rights" has been used by the conservatives to invoke two symbols that tend to overwhelm critical analysis of proposals made in the name of victims. In the criminal law context, the word "victim" has come to mean those who are preyed upon by strangers: "Victim" suggests a nonprovoking individual hit with the violence of "street crime" by a stranger. The image created is that of an elderly person robbed of her life savings, an "innocent bystander" injured or killed during a holdup, or a brutally ravaged rape victim. "Victims" are not prostitutes beaten senseless by pimps or "johns," drug addicts mugged and robbed of their fixes, gang members killed during a feud, or misdemeanants raped by cellmates. Nor does the meaning of "victim" encompass the computer corporation whose trade secrets are stolen or the discount store that suffers petty pilfering. In short, the image of the "victim" has become a blameless, pure stereotype, with whom all can identify. . . .

Compromising Rights

Society has grown tired of the jury trial—the last non-bureaucratic test for truth between the individual and government. . . .

It is as if the criminal justice system is saying:

"The accusation is sufficient. As in *Alice in Wonderland*, first the judgment and then the trial. Let's not waste time on a dispassionate, careful assessment of evidence. Give us coliseum justice."

Thus the rights of both the victim and the accused are sacrified to political exploitation of an oversimplified solution.

John J. Cleary, *USA Today*, April 19, 1984.

"Rights" is also a powerful rhetorical device, particularly in American history and culture. The term suggests both freedom from something and freedom to do something: It suggests a certain vision of independence and autonomy. In the American political context, the word almost automatically raises suspicions of oppression or deprivation and has been called into service by disparate groups seeking power, entitlements, equality, or liberty, often with great success. Hence, the terms "civil rights," "women's rights," "gay rights," "the right to life," and "the right to work" pervade the current political lexicon. Similar force attaches to the concept of "victim's rights." The term has come to mean some undefined, yet irreducible right of crime victims that "trumps" the rights of criminal defendants. Although the rhetoric of proponents of "victim's rights" vacillates between notions of "past victim's rights" and "future victim's rights" without explanation or clarity, the term's predominant meaning in the political context has become that of "future victim's rights."

Unfortunately, the symbolic strength of the term "victim's rights" overrides careful scrutiny: Who could be anti-victim? Thus, liberals find themselves caught in yet another apparent paradox: To be solicitous of a defendant's rights is to be anti-victim. As a result, "victim's rights" has produced an emerging structure of criminal law and procedure that closely resembles the "crime control" model so antithetical to liberal thought. Based on a simplified concept of "victim" and an unarticulated concept of "rights," the changes in the criminal process proposed or spawned by the victim's rights movement are the same changes that have long been advocated by conservatives. Ironically, these changes may do little to help even the very narrow category of past victims who give meaning to the symbol. Moreover, the symbolic manipulation of the victim successfully avoids a more serious debate about how the criminal justice process should be structured and disguises the truly revolutionary nature of the reforms proposed. Whether the reforms have anything to do with victims, and whether they are desirable, are unanswered questions. Upon examination, many of the reforms appear to fail under either line of inquiry. . . .

Victims Must Assume Responsibility

Assuming responsibility for a traumatic experience is a process requiring an assertion or reassertion of control in one's life. Responsibility initially requires an individual to accept that the criminal event occurred. But a frequent first reaction to traumatic experience is a denial that the event occurred at all, in part to avoid the death anxiety produced, but also in part to avoid acknowledgement that such a horrible thing could be a part of life. Yet until the victim acknowledges the actual experience as hers or his alone—that *she* was raped, that *he* was mugged—the victim is virtually powerless to be free from the rapist or the mugger, or to take responsibility for, and thereby reassert control over, the event and the direction of her or his life.

Unfortunately for many crime victims, American culture discourages this kind of personal responsibility and instead emphasizes another type of responsibility—"blame" and fault finding. By blaming others, the victim escapes responsibility. By blaming

153

the victim for his plight, society further discourages the victim from taking responsibility for the event. Accordingly, the societal emphasis on innocence as a prerequisite to being a "real" victim, taken in combination with the confusion between "innocence" and "responsibility," make it very difficult for a victim to avoid displacing the criminal event from her experience. Moreover, the inability of other people, even those close to the victim, to accept the crime victim's experience can further isolate the victim from the experience, thereby blocking successful resolution of the crisis. . . .

Victim's Rights Should Not Subvert the Accused

Although the movement to improve the status of victims in our society has had some success, there is much more to be done. In many ways, the affirmation of the victim's humanity is testimony to a maturing of our society. However, we must resist, at all costs, the temptation to advance the cause of victims by diminishing constitutional rights of the accused. Our purpose instead should be to insure the crime victim's integrity in the justice system without in any way denying constitutional guarantees to the accused.

Morton Bard, *Social Policy*, Winter 1985.

One persistent image of the American criminal process is that it "revictimizes" the victim. The President's Task Force *Final Report*, for example, portrays the ill-treatment of crime victims in a particularly apocryphal story. The *Final Report* describes the insensitive treatment of a widowed 50-year-old rape victim by the police and hospital personnel. It then details the numerous abuses that the criminal justice system inflicted upon the victim, including an indifferent and ineffective attempt at preventing threatening phone calls to the victim by her attacker from jail, an inconvenient scheduling of line-ups, unethical activities by defense counsel, repeated failures by the prosecutor to inform the victim about her role in hearings and the trial and to promptly notify her about postponements, the emotional and financial burden of delays in the process on the victim, the enormous pressure and humiliation of testifying, and the short sentence that was eventually imposed on the rapist.

Horror Stories

The scenario presented in the *Final Report* is indeed horrifying. It is also somewhat incredible to anyone acquainted with criminal law practice, and it is insulting to judges, prosecutors, defense attorneys, and law enforcement officers. It is a composite of everything that could go wrong in the process rather than a chronicle of an actual case. Yet the scenario presented in the *Final Report*, and other horror stories like it, have led to numerous victim's rights proposals that purport to remedy the situation. These proposals typically contain one or more of the following elements:

(a) that the suspect remain in custody after arrest;
(b) that few, if any, delays exist between arrest and preliminary hearing, and between hearing and trial;
(c) that plea bargaining either be eliminated or be victim-determined;
(d) that there be minimal, if any, cross-examination of victims by defense counsel;
(e) that exclusionary rules be abandoned;
(f) that victims be allowed to participate in sentencing;
(g) that victims receive full restitution.

This composite portrays an "ideal" criminal process, one that more closely resembles a model produced by crime control ideology than by supporters of a program designed to spare victims unnecessary trauma. . . .

Focusing on the End of the Justice System

Ironically, the most politically visible activity in the victim's rights movement focuses on the end, rather than on the beginning, of the criminal process. Advocate groups such as MADD attend the sentencings of defendants; formalized victim participation at sentencing frequently appears in victim's rights proposals; and many states have recently adopted provisions allowing victims to participate in sentencing proceedings. . . .

Recent victim's rights proposals appear to be driven more by the retaliatory view of retribution than by the moral aspect of retribution. The victim who participates in sentencing might further the ends of the retribution-as-vengeance theory by providing specific and graphic information about the crime—information that will provoke outrage. . . .

The criminal justice process appears to ignore the concerns, wants, and needs of victims while it simultaneously relies on victims to function. Sacrificing individuals to society's goals seems "unfair" to many; the treatment of victims as a means to an end seems wrong. Victim participation in sentencing ostensibly cures this inequality by giving the victim "equal time." But if fairness or equality are the goals served by participation, waiting until sentencing to recognize the victim does not seem to cure the perceived evil of using the victim as a means to an end. If the real reason for encouraging victims to speak at sentencing is the desire for harsher sentences, the process continues to use the victim for an instrumental purpose. The use of the victim can be more subtle, however, because in many cases the victim participates either to a limited extent, or not at all, after reporting the crime and agreeing to press charges. At best, it may be several months before a sentencing proceeding occurs, assuming that there is a conviction. Thus, the victim may continue to be "used" without fair treatment for an extended period, because sentencing occurs at the end of the criminal process.

Symbolically, the defendant does appear to have an advantage in the criminal process: He has a lawyer, while the victim does not; he enjoys the protection of specific constitutional provisions, while the victim does not; he frequently is the focus of attention and concern—even if that attention and concern are entirely negative in orientation—while attention paid to the victim is typically nonexistent or dependent upon the victim's usefulness to the prosecution. The perception that defendants are somehow advantaged is thus difficult to dispel. The reality, however, is that most defendants have little or no real advantage either substantively or procedurally. And the fact that the defendant has one person ostensibly supporting and advocating his interests—his lawyer—may be considered an advantage by some, but viewed another way, representation is less an advantage than a necessity. Without counsel, the defendant is at a distinct disadvantage in the system; having counsel lessens, but does not obliterate, that disadvantage.

Juries, Not Victims, More Likely To Assure Justice

Another possible argument that can be made in support of victim participation in sentencing is that such participation renders the sentencing process more democratic and thus will make the sentence imposed more reflective of the community's response to a crime. But the fact that democratic legislative bodies set sentences detracts from this argument. Nevertheless, the democratizing function may arguably be better served by allowing the victim and her friends and relatives to participate in sentencing in order to provide the judge with a sense of the community's norms and values in a particular case. The legislature is probably a better measure of those norms and values than is a judge, however, particularly when the judge is faced with a self-selected group of individuals who do not necessarily represent the norms of the community. In fact, if ensuring that community norms prevail is the goal, jury sentencing would be more representative than victim participation. . . .

Concern for Victims or Crime Control?

The concern of this article is to increase the understanding of the experience of victimization, and the manner in which the anguish of victims has been reformulated or mistranslated into support for a particular ideology. The cooptation of victim's concerns by crime control proponents has created a new mythology of victimization that fails to hear those concerns. The following exchange, taken from the Senate Subcommittee Hearings on the

Omnibus Victim and Witness Protection Act, both exemplifies the inability of nonvictims to hear past victims and demonstrates the resulting translation of the anguish of victimization into a condemnation of the offender:

> *Senator Heinz.* Do you have any thoughts on how prosecutors can be more sympathetic or more understanding, more humane in their treatment of people such as yourself?
>
> *Mrs. X.* I certainly do have a lot of opinions. When I talked to the police—I did a series of workshops in the Montgomery County Police Department—the first thing I emphasized was that whether a person is a prosecuting attorney, a judge, or the President of the United States, I would urge him to examine his own feelings about crime. In my particular case, about rape.
>
> What I feel is that most people are so afraid of being victims themselves that when they are dealing with a victim they treat us as anathema. *Our very existence* makes them uncomfortable. I imagine I look like someone you know. Maybe I look like someone you love? I might make you feel uncomfortable just by my existence. Rape happened to me. It wasn't nice. It wasn't midnight, and I wasn't alone or in a bar. I didn't ask for it.
>
> This makes people uncomfortable. I would ask prosecuting attorneys not to hide behind sarcasm here, nor employ the games of the law, not to be afraid of being somehow compassionate, not to confuse cold with professional.
>
> *Senator Heinz.* In other words, what you are really saying is that although the *criminal* may have every step of the way explained to him by his lawyer or, if he can't afford his own lawyer, by a court-appointed lawyer—paid for by the *taxpayer*, there was no one in your case who ever had the courtesy or the simple decency to explain the process and sit down with you and let you know, no matter how uncertain the process was, what it was comprised of.

To whom, or to what, is he responding?

"It is better to defend yourself than bear the humiliation and torture when you don't."

Victims Should Fight Back

Bynum Perkins

One of the many controversial topics in the victims' rights movement is whether or not victims of crime should attempt to defend themselves. Many crime victims purchase weapons, vowing that if a criminal ever attacks them, they will be ready. While the specter of thousands of people walking the streets with hidden guns ready to shoot criminals vigilante-style frightens many people, some believe it is the only way to deter crime. In the following viewpoint, Bynum Perkins, a shopkeeper who shot a burglar during a robbery attempt in his store, argues that this type of action is necessary.

As you read, consider the following questions:

1. How did Perkins' past experience with crime influence his decision to shoot the burglar?
2. Why does Perkins believe that he is not a vigilante?

Bynum Perkins, "Better to Defend Than Bear Humiliation." Reprinted from *U.S. News & World Report*, issue of April 15, 1985. Copyright, 1985, U.S. News & World Report.

What goes through someone's mind when confronted by an armed attacker? Pharmacist Bynum "Doc" Perkins knows the feeling. Robbed several times over the years, the 57-year-old father of six finally decided to fight back when a holdup man entered his store. . . .

I was on the phone to a wholesaler when I heard his voice: "Freeze!" I looked up to find a longhaired man in an Army field jacket pointing an automatic pistol at my head. Instantly, the adrenaline was pumping. While my one hand slowly lowered the phone, the other reached for a gun hidden in a cardboard box. I squeezed the trigger and fired at him.

I hit the man four times, but he never surrendered. Somehow, he managed to limp from the store. The police found him shortly afterward in a flophouse, moaning from his wounds. He pleaded guilty to the crime and was recently sentenced to 20 years in prison.

Anger, Fear, and Humiliation

My response that morning, coldblooded as it may sound, sprang from all the anger, fear and humiliation that had welled up in me over many years.

In the last 25 years, my drugstore on Peachtree Street had been broken into 15 times. In only three of those cases was anyone arrested. Prior to this latest incident, I had been held up at gunpoint twice, and a colleague another time. Other store owners—friends and associates of mine—have been beaten on the head with pistols, shot and even killed. And always I wondered when it would be my turn.

Before, I had been a pushover. I hadn't been hurt physically, but I had been horrified by the robberies. When four other pharmacies in the area were robbed last fall, I prepared myself. I decided that this time I would take a stand if the odds were right. The store would have to be empty of customers, and I would need an element of surprise.

The way it turned out, I know I'm one of the lucky ones. I had never before pointed a gun at anyone, and I shudder and give thanks that I survived. I recall the fear I felt when my gun clicked—out of ammunition—and the man was still able to stand. He could have come back at me. I could have wound up like the young couple in Columbus, Ga., who, not long after my episode, were made to lie down in their store and were shot in the head.

I had been in that same position three years before—on the floor and trembling—when a robber seeking narcotics hit my store. I also know from experience what it is like to see a guy who robbed you out on the street in a matter of months.

Looking back, I have no regrets about the shooting. I've felt better about myself because I fought back.

Someone is going to have to resist somewhere. It is better to defend yourself than bear the humiliation and torture when you don't.

Yet I don't see myself as a vigilante. I didn't take the law into my own hands. I was the victim. Was I supposed to stop and say, "Wait a minute, Mr. Holdup Man, while I call the police?" I'm the last to look for trouble. That man would have been as safe as in his mother's arms if he, like any customer, had paid for his purchase and moved on.

Steve Kelley for the *San Diego Union*. Reprinted with permission.

Still, the tension that such an incident provokes stays with you for a long time. I use a stress thermometer that looks like a plastic credit card. If you're really scared or stressed, it'll register black when pressed against your skin. If you're calm, it'll be blue or green. For two weeks after the last holdup, I was in the black and my heart was beating faster.

One thing that surprised me was the response from other

people—not just here in Atlanta but from all over the country. I guess a thousand people have either phoned me or visited the store to congratulate me. On the back of a dollar bill, one customer wrote, "Bravo, Doc Perkins!" A Louisiana woman wrote: "We have great admiration for you and the subway vigilante who also had the courage to defend himself." Another woman sent a plant and a note that read: "Thank you. I live on the street where they captured the robber."

Some of the assumptions have been disturbing. I've been asked, "Had the man been white, would you still have shot him?" Well, he was white.

Others ask how I can continue to stay in this type of business, convinced as I am that crime keeps getting worse. No one has to tell me that staying here in this location is dangerous, but almost any place in a big city is dangerous. You're in jeopardy waiting for a bus or train in front of your office. You could be mugged or robbed or assaulted.

Besides, this drugstore has been my life and I enjoy it. My customers like me, and I like them. I'd hate to think that I was so weak that I had to run. No matter where I went to open a pharmacy, I'd be taking a chance of getting robbed, not just for the money but for the narcotics.

Bullet Holes a Rabbit Could Jump Through

Despite the risks, I'm happy to come to work every day, and I don't plan to retire anytime soon. But I will always be far more cautious. I catch myself looking up from my work, anxious about who is in the store. It's really ironic. Sometimes I'll wonder what a guy is doing coming in the door, and I have to remind myself that I'm in business to attract customers. My family would like me to hire someone to stay in the store with me, perhaps a security guard, but I can't afford it.

So if it ever happens again, I'll just have to rely upon myself. Last time, I was so unfamiliar with guns that I used the wrong ammunition. My new bullets make a hole big enough for a rabbit to jump through.

"*Robbery attempts actively resisted by their victims were eight to 10 times as likely to result in a victim being killed . . . as when the robbery was not resisted.*"

Victims Should Not Fight Back

Franklin E. Zimring

In December 1984 Bernhard Hugo Goetz became a national celebrity when he shot three young men who attempted to rob him while he was riding a subway. The national media published hundreds of articles and held dozens of press conferences and many experts gave reasons both to support and to decry Goetz's actions. In the following viewpoint, Franklin E. Zimring uses the case to argue that crime victims should not behave as Goetz did. He believes that crime victims who resist are far more likely to be hurt than crime victims who do not. Zimring is acting director of the Earl Warren Legal Institute at the University of California at Berkeley.

As you read, consider the following questions:

1. Why does the author argue that Goetz, unlike most victims, did not run a high risk of being killed?
2. Why does Zimring believe that New York's gun control laws make crime victims safer?
3. For what reason does the author believe Goetz's example is dangerous for society?

Franklin E. Zimring, "Lessons for the Urban Jungle," *Los Angeles Times*, March 15, 1985. Reprinted with permission.

Hero or malefactor, Bernhard Goetz is the benefactor of newspaper editorial pages. . . . Since his New York subway adventure, the mass media have used this incident to illustrate more object lessons than are found in McGuffey's Reader.

The moral instructions . . . derived from the shooting predictably reflect the biases of their authors, and taken together they generate wild contradictions. Depending on your editorial page of choice, this case proves that we need more gun control, that gun control doesn't work or that every law-abiding subway rider should pack a .38. Police presence is either useless or should be doubled. The shooting either threatens the fabric of social control in the city or represents the citizen's only hope because the forces of law and order have already broken down. This case reminds Kenneth Clark that crime is a social disease; it reminds his critics that crime is a sin.

Do Not Resist Robbers

Haven't we heard all this before? We have, and most of the global implications being drawn in the first-round media blitz have been waiting pre-packaged for just this sort of occasion. Yet there are three less ideological, and more modest, lessons to be learned from the . . . facts of the case, and from the growing body of research on violent crime in the United States: (1) Those who become robbery victims should not emulate Goetz and actively resist robbers armed with knives or guns; (2) the specially strict gun control laws that Goetz violated may have saved his life, and (3) the incidence of justifiable homicide, despite its affirmative sound, is a fairly reliable indication of social disease. A high rate of justified killings indentifies a serious problem of violence.

I would urge readers confronted by robbers armed with guns or knives to cooperate with the offender in all but the most unusual circumstances. The life that you save will probably be your own. In a study of robbery in Chicago, James Zuehl and I found that robbery attempts actively resisted by their victims were eight to 10 times as likely to result in a victim being killed (in the street or in a store) as when the robbery was not resisted. With modest amounts of property at stake, this is not a risk worth taking.

For two reasons, however, Goetz did not run an extremely high risk of being killed: He had a gun, and his opponents did not. The latter factor is the most important explanation of his survival.

Having one's own pistol ready to use certainly increases the odds that a crime victim will "win" a confrontation with offenders— and, if widespread, this practice could well decrease the number

of persons willing to try armed robbery. The problem is that while victims might win a greater percentage of battles, the number of victims killed in shoot-outs would increase greatly from the current rate of less than one in 100 gun robberies. Assuming the worst about the four youths involved in the incident, even Wyatt Earp would have had a hard time in a four-on-one gun battle if his opponents had been armed.

But there were no knives or guns on the other side of this confrontation, and that could be why Goetz survived to become a *cause celebre*. In Chicago we found that robbers with guns were three times as likely to kill victims as robbers with knives, and gun robbers were about 20 times as deadly as robbers who use only personal force. These differences in death risk really matter when a victim takes his chances by actively resisting a robber.

Therefore, one can learn a lot about why this victim survived if we find out why his opponents were not armed with deadly weapons. One reason might be that they were not planning to commit robbery. Only a tiny fraction of persons without criminal intentions carry handguns in public places.

Many Robberies Unplanned

But most persons who commit robbery do not arm themselves with guns. Many robberies are unplanned, frighteningly spontaneous recreations that do not result from premeditated armament. Also, the criminal-justice system in New York and everywhere else treats gun robberies more seriously than robbery with other weapons, and this might alter the weapon choice of some confirmed robbers. Further, guns are not instantly available in New York or elsewhere, and are not riskless to carry in violation of both state and local law.

There are two indications that New York's famously ineffective handgun control laws make armed robbery safer for its victims. A smaller percentage of all robberies committed in New York involve guns than in most other cities, and this has been true for decades. Further, the share of robberies committed with guns by teenage offenders in New York is much smaller than that of robberies committed by adult offenders. This seems to be the major reason why adolescent robbers are much less likely to kill their victims. Apparently gun-control laws work (at least on kids), and Goetz may owe his life to the gun law that he violated.

No Cause To Rejoice

I will not venture an opinion here about whether, under New York law, the subway shootings constitute justifiable homicide. It is more important to note that even killings justified by law are no occasion for rejoicing. Some reflection suggests quite the opposite conclusion: A high volume of killings that can be excused because the killer was in fear of his own life is a clear indication of a society in trouble.

This social paradox of justified violence can be simply illustrated. If a man walks into a bar where nobody else has a deadly weapon and kills another, the odds are that a jury will not find that he used lethal force because he reasonably believed that his life was in danger. But if everybody in the bar is armed, we are more likely to conclude that this greater threat justified or excused the lethal act. We excuse the act but do not applaud the result.

No matter the individual justification, the social import of such violence is grim. Bringing your own gun can only be understood as reasonable when circumstances are already deplorable. And the social conditions that justify individual violence announce collective disaster.

Understanding Words in Context

Readers occasionally come across words which they do not recognize. And frequently, because they do not know a word or words, they will not fully understand the passage being read. Obviously, the reader can look up an unfamiliar word in a dictionary. However, by carefully examining the word in the context in which it is used, the word's meaning can often be determined. A careful reader may find clues to the meaning of the word in surrounding words, ideas, and attitudes.

Below are excerpts from the viewpoints in this chapter. In each excerpt, one or two words are printed in italics. Try to determine the meaning of each word by reading the excerpt. Under each excerpt you will find four definitions for the italicized word. Choose the one that is closest to your understanding of the word.

Finally, use a dictionary to see how well you have understood the words in context. It will be helpful to discuss with others the clues which helped you decide on each word's meaning.

1. When we try to fit the equal-treatment for the victim *PRECEPT* into a judicial system that wisely refuses to consider anyone a criminal until proven guilty, we run into problems.

   PRECEPT means:
   a) principle
   b) requirement
   c) accusation
   d) desire

2. The tension that a robbery *PROVOKES* stays with you for a long time.

   PROVOKES means:
   a) ends
   b) prod
   c) causes
   d) decides

3. Hero or *MALEFACTOR*, Bernhard Goetz is the *BENEFACTOR* of newspaper editorial pages.

MALEFACTOR means:
a) hero
b) evil-doer
c) male hormone
d) diseased person

BENEFACTOR means:
a) wrongdoer
b) a giver to charity
c) one who benefits
d) anarchist

4. The reason Goetz survived his attack and became a *CAUSE CELEBRE* is because his attackers were not armed.

CAUSE CELEBRE means:
a) a well-known incident
b) festive occasion
c) a face in the crowd
d) survivor

5. No matter what the individual justification, the social *IMPORT* of such violence is grim.

IMPORT means:
a) taboo
b) foreign products brought to the US
c) meaning
d) blunder

6. Although victims' rights may be viewed as a popular movement, genuine questions about victims and victimization have become *COOPTED* by conservatives to support their own cause.

COOPTED means:
a) adopted
b) popularized
c) avoided
d) left over

7. The overwhelming sympathy *EVOKED* by the term "victims' rights" overrides careful *SCRUTINY* of its meaning.

EVOKED means:
a) implied
b) understood
c) stopped
d) called forth

SCRUTINY means:
a) glance
b) examine
c) understanding
d) knowledge

8. Because of our discomfort with the issue of crime, society tends to treat its victims as *ANATHEMA*.

ANATHEMA means:
a) helpless
b) a curse
c) a delight
d) a burden

Periodical Bibliography

The following list of periodical articles deals with the subject matter of this chapter.

John R. Anderson and Paul L. Woodard	"Victim and Witness Assistance: New State Laws and the System's Response," *Judicature*, December/January 1985.
Charles Ansell	"I Can Kill You—My Life Hung on a Stranger's Boast," *Los Angeles Times*, January 10, 1985.
A. Ashworth	"Punishment and Compensation: Victims, Offenders and the State," *Oxford Journal of Legal Studies*, Spring 1986.
Steven Berglas	"Why Did this Happen to Me?" *Psychology Today*, February 1985.
Warren T. Brookes	Is there a Case for Vigilantism?" *Human Events*, April 6, 1985.
Lynne H. Herrington	"The Victim of Crime," *South Texas Law Journal*, Summer 1985.
Donald Lambro	"Real Help for Crime Victims," *Conservative Digest*, April 1985.
J. Anthony Lucas	"When a Citizen Fights Back," *Parade Magazine*, September 8, 1985.
Peter Michelmore	"Could They Forgive Their Son's Killer?" *Reader's Digest*, May 1986.
R.J. Miner	"Victims and Witnesses: New Concerns in the Criminal Justice System," *New York Law School Law Review*, 1985.
Salim Muwakkil	"Crime: Is Self-Defense the Best Defense?" *In These Times*, February 6-12, 1985.
The Nation	"Mean-Streak Culture," January 12, 1985.
Roger A. Pauley	"The Emerging 'Victim Factor' in the Supreme Court's Criminal Jurisprudence: Should Victims' Interests Ever Prevent a Court from Overturning a Conviction?" *Indiana Law Journal*, Spring 1986.
Arnold Rosenblat	"Making Fear Work for You," *USA Today*, July 1985.
Margaret Steinfels	"Fear and Revenge: Personal Perspective," *Christianity and Crisis*, March 4, 1985.

Are Lawyers Ethical?

"Lawyers know that no other group or profession sets higher ethical standards, disciplines itself so rigorously, [and] contributes so much unpaid service to the public."

Lawyers Have High Ethical Standards

David R. Brink

David R. Brink is president of the American Bar Association. In the following viewpoint, he argues that lawyers are unfairly criticized for being unethical. Ultimately, he believes, lawyers cannot work to make themselves loved, but rather must work for their love of law.

As you read, consider the following questions:

1. How does the author explain the discrepancy between people's general opinion of lawyers and their opinion of lawyers with whom they have had personal experiences?
2. Who, according to Brink, punishes the unethical lawyer?
3. Does the author believe that lawyers should seek approval by the public? Why or why not?

David R. Brink, "The Image, the Truth, and the Bard," *ABA Journal*, May 1982. Reprinted with permission from the *ABA Journal*, The Lawyer's Magazine.

Because I believe so strongly in law, lawyers, and the policies of this Association, I try . . . "to answer vigorously every unjust criticism and remedy every justifiable complaint." In the next sentence I added that I would address the "image of lawyers . . . another day." For those in search of buried announcements, this is that day.

Lawyers in court or in negotiations need to worry about the client's image; perhaps that is why we worry so much about our own. "Image" is a modern concept, and its modern measure is polls—public opinion surveys. Polls can be found that prove almost anything, depending on who is surveyed and how the questions are framed. As applied to lawyers, the most consistent poll results are that lawyers in general receive a low confidence rating, but individual lawyers who are known or used by those surveyed, enjoy a high rating. That seeming paradox can be explained only by the fact that opinions of lawyers in general—the lawyers one does not know—are molded by books, periodicals, newspapers, television, radio, movies; broadly defined, the media. This casts a heavy burden on the media to report fully and fairly, and on our profession to emphasize the truth about lawyers, courts, and law. That is why I answer columnists—against the odds.

High Ethical Standards

Lawyers know that no other group or profession sets higher ethical standards, disciplines itself so rigorously, contributes so much unpaid service to the public, or labors so tirelessly for the improvement of the justice system and society. At times it seems to lawyers as though the old saw "No news is good news" were read by reporters as "Good news is no news." There *is* a "man bites dog" quality about the unusual case where the man or woman of justice—the lawyer or judge—is found dramatically unjust that makes it newsworthy. But lawyers often look in vain to find in print that it is our profession itself that uncovers and disciplines the occasional wrongdoing lawyer or makes good the rare defalcation. And we seldom read in the public press of our programs to enhance lawyer competence and ethics, reduce court costs and delay, promote dispute resolution, improve substantive and procedural law, and provide services to the poor at no cost and to others at affordable prices.

Yet there are signs that media coverage of law and lawyers is becoming fairer and more complete. The profession, led by this Association, more than ever is addressing itself to the public interest, and that fact is not passing unnoticed by reporters. Many reporters now are specializing in legal matters and the accuracy

171

and balance of legal reporting are improving rapidly.

Perhaps most significantly, the public and the media are currently fascinated by law and lawyers. The actions of our citizens speak louder than their words of response to pollsters. It seems as though everyone wants to go to law school. Everyone wants to sue his or her neighbor, an institution, or the government. Even mediocre books about lawyers, courts, or law become instant bestsellers. The courtroom scene and the lawyer as hero or villain are high points of television and the movies. National periodicals proclaim this "The Age of the Lawyer." The fascination may be a love-hate relationship, but it is bringing home to the media that the good news about lawyers is newsworthy, as well as the bad.

Scorning Lawyers, an American Pastime

Medicine has a morally directing goal: health. The controlling objective of the law is justice. It is served, not mocked, by an adversary process because that process has evolved an elegant ethic of reasonableness, and professional standards of due process in serving clients.

Looking down on others is the lazy person's path to self-esteem. Scorning lawyers is a luxury enjoyed by persons whose moral self-satisfaction derives from living down to standards less exacting than those by which most lawyers strive to live.

George F. Will, *Minneapolis Star and Tribune*, September 20, 1986.

So our image may not be as negative as we fear. And I suggest that, ultimately, lawyers must seek, as their goal and satisfaction, not love of being loved, but love of law. For so long as lawyers deal often with claims to money or property, charge fees—however justified, function in an adversary system that produces both winners and losers, and pursue the great tradition of defending even unpopular persons and causes, lawyers can expect public love only up to a point. If we have not yet reached that point, we can merely be patient and love what we do in our noblest of callings.

Quotations on Lawyers

Nearly every published attack on lawyers includes an ancient or modern quotation, or misquotation. Usually it is the line from Shakespeare: "The first thing we do, let's kill all the lawyers." Shakespeare was wiser than those who borrow his words today. For in his play the line was spoken by one who was plotting how to overthrow the government. Shakespeare understood that the bulwark of an orderly society is its legal profession.

"The excesses of today's legal system and those who profess to be its servants in fact amount to a serious problem and are at the root of a festering public disrespect for the law."

Lawyers Are More Concerned with Money than Ethics

Samuel Jan Brakel

Samuel Jan Brakel is a research attorney for the American Bar Foundation. In the following viewpoint, Brakel argues that current lawyer publications reveal an overriding concern with making money. The public has a bad view of lawyers for good reason, he believes. Attorneys should make a greater attempt to police themselves.

As you read, consider the following questions:

1. Why does Brakel argue that most lawyers believe they are getting a bum rap from the public and media? Does he think this is an accurate perception?
2. What cases does the author cite to prove his claim that lawyers are greedy?
3. What does Brakel believe should be done to improve lawyers' professionalism?

Samuel Jan Brakel, "ProSe," *Student Lawyer*, February 1986, Vol. 14, No. 6. Reprinted with the author's permission.

Lawyers historically have not had good press. From Shakespeare to Dickens to today's mere mortal critics (Jethro Leiberman, Jerold Auerbach), the next-most ancient profession has come in for some truly scathing commentary. "Litigious" and "belegaled" are the terms used most often today to depict the plight of a society—modern western society in particular—whose citizens seem to be at the persistently untender mercies of hordes of lawyers out to sell them their legal snake oil, anxious to dupe all into pursuing factious and frivolous claims, and ever ready to ply their technicalities to subvert justice and exonerate those who deserve the worst. Its longevity alone suggests that there must be considerable truth to the complaint: in seducing clients to purchase their wares and in pandering an ever-expanding array of legal rights and rites, lawyers too often, too closely, resemble those who service the public in the one profession that pre-dates the legal trade.

Half-Hearted Pummeling

It should come as no surprise that only few in the legal profession believe this baleful barrage of criticism to be deserved. Most lawyers don't really see there is a problem. To be sure, like many an organized group, we in the profession engage in periodic breast-beating, but it is a very restrained and half-hearted pummeling we administer. On predictable occasions a voice from the wilderness (of bar association meetings) expresses concern about inadequacies in lawyer competence or ethics, about court delays and judicial overload, but these exercises appear to be largely symbolic, operating within the safe margins of professional self-regard. Basically, we remain convinced that the more there is of law (and lawyers) the better. Making one's contribution to the proliferation of legal rights is still a sacred goal. We commission research studies and appoint committees to prove to ourselves that the legal needs of the public will always be with us, infinite and unmet. And rather than acknowledge the law's limits in redressing every social ill or personal grievance, we talk instead about the continuing need to provide more and better "access" to the legal system.

Most recently, even our critics have become our apologists. Researchers who used to see capitalist conspiracy and exploitation in every corner of the law have of late helped salve our collective professional conscience with the "objective" finding that there really is no litigation explosion in our land after all. The vast majority of disputes never reach the courts; most of those that do are settled before trial. The legal profession is merely respon-

174

sive and mostly responsible. The alarm is false. This isn't *Bleak House* 1985. We ought not "kill all the lawyers" just yet. All is right with the world.

It Just Ain't So

Comforting as this may sound, the trouble is that it just ain't so. All is not right with the legal world. The excesses of today's legal system and those who profess to be its servants in fact amount to a serious social problem and are at the root of a festering public disrespect for the law and diminishing confidence in its institutions. The crux of the problem is as much qualitative—to what uses the law is being put—as one of quantitative overuse. And the evidence is all around us: in the morning papers, on the radio talk shows, the evening television news—wherever we choose to get our media fix—not to mention in our tax bills, professional service fees, insurance premiums, and so forth.

"Of course there are a lot of lawyers.
There are just as many criminals."

The profession's case is not helped by what we find in the legal journals, including its avowedly mainstream publications. Indeed, the evidence of the law's overreaching often lies there in Augena concentrations: one encounters example after example of lawyers caught up in the unbridled pursuit of consumer "need" that is provider-created, each of them energetically chasing after the big and ever-bigger buck, and all of it piously presented as a matter of cloaking the otherwise legally naked citizen in his God-given, inalienable rights.

Take, for example, a few articles that ran last year in the *ABA Journal*, the bar's official organ. In the March 1985 issue, the *Journal* presented a brief piece on the legal fallout from the 1979 DC-10 air crash in Chicago. The fact that this crash, killing 271 people, was one of the worst in aviation history is not what makes it newsworthy for a legal journal. Human tragedy routinely provides the setting for the work of lawyers. The bigger the tragedy, the greater the number of potential clients, the bigger the stakes, and the more lawyers will enter the legal fray. The *Journal*'s angle on the story is that Aaron Broder, the lawyer for one of the deceased passengers, has managed to obtain for his "client" in a suit brought in a federal district court in New York, a $10,000 award for "pre-impact pain and suffering," allegedly incurred during the three seconds that the aircraft nosedived to the ground after losing one of its wing engines.

Damage Awards for the Dead

Now the very notion that dead persons can be lawyers' clients and collect damages from the so-called parties at fault may strike the ordinary person as curious. What is the point? Who benefits? As properly schooled lawyers, however, we no longer bat an eye. Immersed in the nether-world of estates, survivors, and testators, we can accept the fact that even if money can't bring back the dead, it can accomplish about everything else—redeem the latent liabilities of the estate, meet the financial obligations of the survivors, heal the psychic wounds of the next-of-kin, satisfy the greed that even the bereft are not free of, and line the pockets of the lawyers who choose to represent these various "interests." But $10,000 for three seconds of presumed mental pain immediately preceding death (added to various other compensatory awards)— that, even to the initiated, begins to sound like extraordinarily creative reparations work. . . .

There is also, for example, in the February [1985] issue of the *Journal* a brief report on the Jordan, Minnesota child sexual abuse case which notes that the attorney for one of the families originally implicated in the scandal is suing the county for a paltry $34 million. A less restrained lawyer for another family, according to the story, is asking for $100 million. If this is "justice" for the victimized, as the lawyers argue, then the lady does not come cheap. One could run for a year close to half this nation's legal services-for-the-poor programs on that kind of money. Later, we read about a medical malpractice settlement that guarantees the plaintiff—a boy who suffered brain damage while undergoing treatment for a respiratory disease—a minimum of $26 million which could, with passing years of the boy's life, rise to $120 million. If the defendants were willing to settle for that, one wonders what the plaintiff's lawyer initially asked for or how high a jury might have gone. The argument from economics that seeks to rationalize these results centers on the presumed deterrent effect of such judgments. Doctors faced with potential penalties of that order for malpractice will, it is said, make sure to perform up to snuff. The alternate possibility is, of course, that such judgments will deter the smocks right off them.

When "the Fun Begins"

Following the above is a brief blurb on lawyers who specialize in bill collecting for business clients. It quotes one of them—in a caption below his photograph—as saying that turning a judgment into money is when "the fun begins." No doubt there is need for orderly processes to get debtors and deadbeats to pay up, and one surmises that lawyers are as well-positioned and well-oriented as any group, and better than most, to be involved in this unpleasant business. It is, however, hardly the kind of work that should be highlighted with such unsuppressed glee. A couple of pages later, in a regular section of quotable "Quotes" from the legal front, we are given this one-liner from a New York City labor lawyer on the problem of increasing white-collar layoffs: "Of course, these layoffs are all good for the lawyers." Possibly refreshing in isolation, such candor here only echoes as the stale refrain of lawyerly self-seeking. It is an echo that reverberates in another story reporting that a New York appellate court has held unconstitutional (as violating the right to free speech) the state's long-standing prohibition against lawyers' solicitation of accident victims by mail. This is the age of reform. The time for stuffy, antiquated notions of professional propriety is up. All hail the First Amendment! What's the zip code for Bhopal? Mexico City? Armero?

The suspicion that self-interest is dominant contaminates even lawyers' loftier pursuits, as in a piece by Ralph Nader and an attorney with Nader's Public Citizen Litigation Group entitled "Public Interest Law with Bread on the Table." It informs us that there are today more than 100 federal statutes which allow prevailing plaintiffs to recover their attorney's fees from the defendant (typically a government official or agency) and that the courts have been approving some very hefty fees indeed in cases of this kind. Lawyers thus seem to be well on their way to accomplishing the proverbial impossible—that one can get rich doing good. Whether everyone's definition of "good" squares with Mr. Nader's, or with the premises implied in any or most of the legal actions brought under these statutes, is something else again.

The temptation is to throw up one's hands, to sputter about the complexity of things and how deeply ingrained in our general culture the excesses of the legal system are. No doubt true. At the same time, there are things that can be done. On the specific or "micro-level," if you will, judges have wide-ranging authority to cut into the problem. They have discretion to reduce jury awards. They can throw out cases that do not present a "legally cognizable" (read: reasonable) cause. Claims that strike the court as exceptionally pernicious or farfetched can be dismissed as being "against public policy." And there are even sanctions that can be applied against parties and counsel who bring false or frivolous suits. All we need then are wise and courageous judges to do these things.

Confusion Over Lawyers' Role

The key to understanding this confusion—if not entirely dispelling it—is to grasp a basic truth. Lawyers and law firms are businesses, and their business is conflict. Creative lawyering often means exploiting or creating conflicts. Just as companies develop new products, so lawyers search for new legal theories on which to sue. Rights of action are lawyers' markets. But their economic self-interest—their legal innovations—may subvert their social usefulness. The civil-justice system's essential purpose is to resolve conflict, not to excite it.

It's often a pretense that lawyers represent other people's grievances rather than their own economic interests. There are thousands of cases where lawyers, not their supposed clients, are the main aggressors.

Robert J. Samuelson, *Newsweek*, March 10, 1986.

They won't, of course, not enough of them, not without a great deal more outside support than is presently there for it. This is where the need for change on the "macro-level" comes in. It is time for the profession itself to expose the excesses of the law for what they are and to publicize the damage that self-seeking, over-reaching, lawyers do to public confidence in the legal system. It is time to enlist that vastly larger number of lawyers whose work consists of providing needed, reasonable services in the effort to weed out the instances and elements of excessive lawyering, an effort that must begin at the roots by eliminating the material and psychological profit that has long been available for it. Success in this venture, if it comes, will not come overnight. But that does not absolve us from trying or making a start. Whether or not we ever get close to creating a form of legal heaven that genuinely serves the public's interest, we may at least reap some credit for having paved the road to that other place for those within the profession who are wont to sneer at its better intentions.

178

"If the government doesn't prove its case, the accused should go free."

The Case for Defending the Guilty

James S. Kunen

In the debate over lawyers and criminals' rights, many critics argue that lawyers manipulate and confuse the jury, which results in guilty criminals receiving light sentences. In the following viewpoint, James S. Kunen defends the lawyer's responsibility to aid a guilty client. By describing one of his cases in which he defends an obviously guilty client, Kunen argues that unless the prosecutor can prove beyond a reasonable doubt a criminal is guilty, an attorney should do everything possible to convince the jury to acquit. Kunen lives in New York City, where he has temporarily given up law for writing.

As you read, consider the following questions:

1. What defense does Kunen finally devise to defend his client?
2. Why do you think Kunen is proud of his role in the justice system?
3. Do you think the jury was right in this case? Why or why not?

Croft's chair grudgingly harumphed back, its legs scoring the linoleum. He swore to tell the truth, the whole truth, and nothing but the truth, so help him God, and took the stand. He was completely calm. He answered my questions coolly—a little too coolly, in fact. He didn't have the proper affect. He should have been a little upset that his wife was gone, maybe a little sorry that a man was dead, certainly a little nervous that he was facing life imprisonment. He was none of these, nor was he, on the other hand, cocky or bitter. He was nothing. (The one adjective that perhaps fit him was "rehearsed," as one observer put it. Maybe we had fallen into the trap of overpreparation. On the other hand, we didn't want any screw-ups.)

We eased into the testimony in the traditional manner: What's your name? Age? Job? Where do you live? How long have you lived there? Do you live with anyone? And that brought up the story of his life with the lovely Arlene Croft, and a touching story it was.

"Did you ask her out the first time you met her?"

"No."

"Why not?"

Croft hung his head for half a beat. "I was bashful, I guess. I had to get my courage up."

And on to the happy marriage, the two children, and then the *crime*. The *crime*, of course, was Sales's affair with Arlene. That was well-established.

That crime ruined Croft's life. It had led inexorably to his sitting in this court, accused of murder. How Croft had suffered! He was so upset that he raised his hand against his wife, actually *struck* her, on three different occasions.

He was telling everything. He was making a clean breast of it. He testified that he really *had* carried Daniels's pistol around, because he was nervous after the burglary of his home. And yes, he kept the money for himself after he sold the pistol to the manager of the Cannery Row Club five days before the shooting because he was in debt, because of his auto accident.

On November 14, Croft said, he got a phone call from Sales, went for a brooding walk, and went to talk to him. "Sales said, 'I told you if you brought your ass around me again I'd blow your . . . head off!'"

Contradictory Testimony

Croft described how he took the gun from Sales, exactly as he had explained it to me and to Detective Luce. Then, "He lunged at me, and I was afraid he'd get the gun back and kill me. I fired."

"How many shots did you fire?"

180

"I don't know, two or three."

Two or three? Well, he didn't *exactly* contradict his statement to Detective Luce about putting two shots into Sales on the floor, and the prosecutors didn't attempt to impeach him with that prior inconsistent statement.

Captain Biscet didn't lay a glove on Croft in cross-examination, so the judge tag-teamed with her. It's unfair, but common, for the judge to conduct examinations for the prosecution. It gives the jury the idea that the judge, in his wisdom, wants the prosecution to win, for some reason. But judges call it "assisting in the search for truth," and appellate courts aren't offended by it unless the judge goes completely overboard.

Exploring Human Nature

Strange as it may seem, I grew to like to defend men and women charged with crime. It soon came to be something more than winning or losing a case. I sought to learn why one man goes one way and another takes an entirely different road. I became vitally interested in the causes of human conduct. This meant more than the quibbling with lawyers and juries, to get or keep money for a client so that I could take part of what I won or saved for him: I was dealing with life, with its hopes and fears, its aspirations and despairs. With me it was going to the foundation of motive and conduct and adjustments for human beings, instead of blindly talking of hatred and vengeance, and that subtle, indefinable quality that men call "justice" and of which nothing really is known.

Clarence Darrow, 1932.

"How come Sales ended up on his back if he was lunging forward?" the judge wanted to know.

"I don't know. Maybe it was the force of the shots."

Plausible.

"What was the pattern of the shots?" The judge was leaning over the bench looking down at Croft.

"BANG." Pause. "BANGBANGBANG." The pause was the important part. That's when the gun was changing hands.

"If it was Sales's gun, why didn't you keep it?"

"I was afraid. I wasn't thinking." Croft was sitting forward in the witness chair, looking straight up at the judge, three feet away.

"This man you said you sold Daniels's gun to—did you try to find him to come and testify?"

"I've been in pretrial confinement since November fourteenth, sir."

"Did you have your lawyers try?"

"I object, Your Honor!" I said as I leapt to my feet. "As the court

181

knows, the defense asked for continuance and for funds for investigators. . . ."

"All right. All right," the judge said and left off questioning. . . .

The Closing Argument

The more I reviewed the evidence, the more despondent I became. We had an insoluble problem, and it was the same problem we were aware of on day one: Croft's story was inherently incredible. He borrows Daniels's gun, which is the type of gun which fired the fatal bullets, and that gun is nowhere to be found. He says he sold it *five days* before the shooting, but he never told Daniels he sold it, never gave him the money, and the buyer can't be found. He says he pulled Sales's gun away from Sales and fired in self-defense, but the autopsy suggests at least one shot went into Sales as he lay on the floor. Then he threw Sales's gun, the one piece of evidence that could exonerate him, into the Potomac. As against that pyramid of improbabilities, the government's theory was simple and had no loose ends: Croft brought Daniel's gun with him, blew Sales away, and threw the gun into the river. All the jury had to decide was, *whose gun was in the Potomac?* And the answer seemed as obvious as it was damning.

Even as I realized that the events of November 14 did not look good, I was swept over by another realization: the events of February 25 through 28, in the courtroom, *had* looked good. We had put on a much slicker presentation than the prosecution had.

"Put the government on trial!" I exclaimed aloud. Get the jury to *forget* about November 14, and concentrate on the events that had transpired in the courtroom, the events that they had *seen*, the events that were most *real* to them. The prosecution had been slipshod; the prosecution had not done its job; the prosecution did not *deserve* to win. Couple that with our theme from the beginning—Sales deserved to die—and we just might win.

I put together an overview of the trial from that perspective. By 3:00 A.M. I had eight yellow legal pad pages filled with an outline. I was as prepared as I was going to be. I drove home and slept two hours. . . .

Before the Jury

The time came that I was standing in the center of the court, spectators behind me, the jury towering over me. I heard my quavering voice. I had begun.

"Your Honor, ladies and gentlemen of the court: first of all, we want to thank you for your attention during what has been a long, and not always fascinating, trial. I think we all know better now what is meant by 'a trying experience.'" Clunk. *God, where is my judgment? But seriously, folks. . . .*

I went into the standard burden-of-proof rap, with a little extra emphasis on the patriotism angle. "This is the last opportunity I'm going to have to speak to you on behalf of Peter Croft. I talk only once. The prosecutor gets to speak again. And there's a reason for that. It's not just some technicality or rule of procedure. The government gets to speak again because of a principle which is the very foundation of our whole system of law; a principle upon which this nation was founded; a principle which distinguished our country from most of the nations of the earth [the jurors sat taller and seemed to fight back the urge to salute], and that is, that the government has the burden of proving, beyond a reasonable doubt, that the citizen accused is guilty of each and every element of the offense. Peter Croft is presumed innocent. He didn't even have to testify.''. . .

"The government is *accusing* Peter Croft of murdering Sales." (I had decided to use Croft's first and last name every time I mentioned him, and to use Sales's last name only, in order to humanize the one, dehumanize the other, and most important, to try to keep myself from calling one by the other's name, which I had done at least once a day from the beginning.)

Why Defend the Guilty?

It is dirty work but someone must do it. We cannot have a functioning adversary system without a partisan for both sides. The defense counsel's job is no different and the work no more despicable than that of the lawyer in a civil case, who arranges, argues, and even orients the facts with only the client's interest in mind. . . .

The criminally accused are the representatives of us all. When their rights are eroded, the camel's nose is under and the tent may collapse on anyone. In protecting the constitutional rights of the accused, we are only protecting ourselves.

Barbara Allen Babcock, *Stanford Lawyer,* Spring 1984.

"There's no question that Sales is dead, and there is no question that Peter Croft fired the shots that killed him. The question is, was the killing wrongful, that is, was it murder? Or was there legal justification for it, that is, was it self-defense?

"How will you decide that question? The one way you will *not* decide it is the way the prosecutor said." A few jurors followed my example as I cast a sidelong glance at Captain Biscket, who was pretending to be busy writing. "She said, 'We can only *speculate* as to what happened.' [She actually said that.] As the judge will instruct you, *speculate* is one thing you will not do. We do not decide issues on speculation, but by considering the evidence.

"What did the evidence show? Remember, we presented an

opening statement in which we outlined for you what we expected the testimony would be, *before* the first witness took the stand." I recapitulated the opening statement, painting yet again the picture of the gun-toting Sales, home-wrecker, braggert, sexist, a man "looking over his shoulder" because he knew what he deserved. "And isn't that exactly what the testimony was? How could Peter Croft have known what all those witnesses would say before they said it? There's only one way: Peter Croft knew what they would say because he knew they would tell the truth, just as *he* told you the truth." (This was one inference supported by the evidence, and it was permissible for me to argue it to the jury. I was under no obligation to point out other, equally permissible inferences, such as that our investigators had interviewed most of the witnesses, or that we had the prior sworn statements of all of them.)

So much for the trial of Peter Croft; now for the trial of the government.

"The government, in its closing, misstated Dr. Korzeniewski's testimony. The prosecutor said that Dr. Korzeniewski said that Sales's arm was stretched to the side, not lunging forward. You remember what Dr. Korzeniewski *really* said. He said, 'I can't determine what particular position his arm was in.' The government tried to distort the testimony, tried to fool you. And I ask you, as calmly as I can, with all the control over my voice that I can muster, 'Isn't that *reprehensible?* Don't you have the right to expect better than that from your government?' " To my own surprise, my voice shook with genuine rage as I pointed an accusing finger at Captain Biscket. She looked down at her notepad.

The Coroner's Testimony

I had my own plan for the coroner's testimony. "Let's pretend for a moment that the lieutenant colonel [sitting in the jury's center seat] is Peter Croft, backing out the door, and I am Sales." I lunged toward her. "POW!" I held my pen to my lip at the angle of the bullet's trajectory and jerked my face to the right, as though from the impact of the bullet. "The first shot enters above the lip, travels left to right, front to back, upward. It's fatal. POW! The second shot, left to right, slightly upward, penetrating the left shoulder, passing through the armpit, upward, cuts the trachea and subclavian artery and drops into the chest. Fatal." I spun to my right as I said this. "POW! Number three. Through the left arm. Flesh wound. POW! Four, left to right, through the musculature, making an oval exit as though the back were on the floor; it causes no serious injury."

Now they'd *seen* that it happened just as Peter Croft had described it.

"Finally, the government called Mr. Strickland, the firearms expert. And the goverment elicited testimony from him at great length, just as though he had something material to say. But he really didn't, did he? The government was trying to do it with mirrors, make it seem as though he were saying something he never said. When the smoke cleared, what exactly had he said?

"He testified that *among* the *suspect* weapons are thirty-eight and three-fifty-seven Magnum revolvers manufactured by Rohm, RG Industries, Charter Arms, Dickson, Burgo, Liberty Arms, and Ruger [Sales's brand]. Each manufacturer makes different models, and each model has a production run of individual weapons. If Mr. Strickland's testimony had been the same, but translated in terms of cars, then what he said would have been: 'The suspect car was a compact or a subcompact. Among the suspect manufacturers are Honda, Toyota, Datsun, Subaru, Chevy, Ford, Plymouth, or Mercury.'

"Peter Croft told you that he went to Philadelphia and sold Daniels's weapon to the bouncer at the Cannery Row Club. Did the government adduce any evidence to the contrary? Did they show that Peter Croft was on duty that weekend? That the Cannery Row Club doesn't exist?

"*Everything* happened just like Peter Croft told you. And he doesn't have to prove *anything*. The *government* has to prove, beyond a reasonable doubt, that Peter Croft wrongfully killed Sales. And the government hasn't proven *anything!* . . .

The Jury Reaches a Verdict

Before we had a chance to reflect, we were called back to the courtroom. Forty-five minutes had passed. After evaluating the testimony of thirty-three witnesses, the jurors were back with their verdict. The "president of the court" (foreman), a John Wayne look-alike lieutenant colonel, stood and, grim-faced, with a faltering voice, read the following: "The court, two thirds of all members present concurring in each finding of guilty, finds the defendant: of the charge, not guilty; of the specification, not guilty; of the additional charge, guilty; of the additional specification, guilty." Not guilty of murder, guilty of carrying an unregistered firearm. The jury, which had been unanimous in both findings, pronounced sentence: ten days' incarceration, with credit for ninety days he had served in pretrial detention. Croft was a free man.

Croft smiled and shook my hand. "I never doubted for a second that we were going to win," he said. "Can I get my shotgun back?"

Croft's guards threw their arms around him.

The judge came up to me in the hallway. "If you'd like, I'll give you that continuance now," he said, smiling. Judges like it when the best lawyering wins—they're lawyers, too.

"'Getting away with murder,'" I thought, upon hearing the verdict. "I have *gotten away with murder.*" I was awed by the *enormity* of it. The Sixth Commandment. It made me feel bad—my stomach, particularly—but not as bad as *losing* would have. To those turkeys? Yet another client of mine locked up? I preferred to grapple with the moral problem of winning. That's the sort of problem you want to have.

Anyway, I really didn't know whether Croft had committed murder. There was certainly some evidence to suggest that he had, but, on the other hand, how account for the wild shot high in the wall? Why would he pick the middle of the afternoon in a public lobby in front of a video camera? In any case, it didn't matter what I thought.

Asked by Boswell what he thought of "supporting a cause which you know to be bad," Dr. Johnson replied, "Sir, you do not know it to be good or bad till the Judge determines it. . . . An argument which does not convince yourself, may convince the Judge to whom you urge it: and if it does convince him, why, then, Sir, you are wrong, and he is right." Dr. Johnson's observation is reprinted in the A.B.A. *Code of Professional Responsibility.*

Croft was not guilty. The jury said so.

Regardless of what Croft had or had not done, there remained the problem of what I had done in preparing him to testify. A popular handbook for defense attorneys reflects the mainstream thinking of the defense bar when it suggests, "Although he should not tell the witness specifically what to say, it is certainly within the province of counsel to discuss the witness's answers, highlighting possible problems with proposed answers and suggesting ways in which they could be avoided. The witness should also be instructed as to any potential pitfalls in his testimony and how best to deal with them." . . .

Better To Be Overzealous

I do think it's better to be overzealous than underzealous. Overzealousness can be corrected by the prosecution. (They might at least have asked, "Did you go over your testimony with your attorney?" an innocent question with an innocent answer—"Yes"— but one that nonetheless communicates a certain suspicion to the jury.) Underzealousness cannot be corrected by anyone.

An hour after the verdict, the defense team—not including Croft, who'd gone back to be processed out of the stockade—sat around the kitchen table in Captain Arnold's Florida Avenue row house, drinking Scotch and champagne and smoking. We relived the trial amid gales of laughter, the responsibility off our shoulders and our hearts exultant—we were the victors.

"I couldn't believe it when you said, 'Maybe the Cannery Row Club doesn't exist'!" Arnold laughed.

"I didn't realize I said that."

"It didn't matter *what* you said. You were *rolling,* and the jury was rolling with you."

As my mood got more and more elevated, it dawned on me that

186

my patriotic rap to the jury about the United States' being different from most of the nations of the world, because we put the burden of proof on the government, was *true*. I had thought I was being cynical and manipulative when I'd said it, but it really was true. And if the government doesn't prove its case, the accused *should* go free.

I felt proud to be an American. . . .

The Need for Smart Criminal Lawyers

"If the courts were organized to promote justice," Clarence Darrow told the inmates of the Cook County Jail in 1902, "the people would elect somebody to defend all the criminals *[sic]*, somebody as smart as the prosecutor—and give him as many detectives and as many assistants to help, and pay as much money to defend you as to prosecute you."

Darrow's vision will probably never be fully realized, as justice is never as popular as order. Still, Darrow would have been impressed by the system in Washington, D.C., where the courts operate in a reasonably just fashion: most of the guilty are convicted, and nearly all of the innocent go free. . . .

The courts cannot reduce crime or establish justice. They are just a sorting mechanism between the front end of the system— the police—and the back end—the prisons. To the extent that the public supports adequate judicial resources and effective representation for the accused, the sorting can be done in a just and equitable manner.

I am proud of the role I played in that process.

"I could no longer cope with the ugliness and brutality that had for so long, too long, been a part of my life."

The Case Against Defending the Guilty

Seymour Wishman

Seymour Wishman has practiced criminal law in New York and New Jersey for both the defense and the prosecution. In 1977 he served as Deputy Assistant to the President. In the following viewpoint, Wishman questions his role in the criminal justice system. He discusses his involvement in a particularly heinous case that resulted in a minor sentence for a guilty man. Wishman questions the nature of a system that can reward his peculiar ability to defend the guilty.

As you read, consider the following questions:

1. When does the author realize that his professional detachment has become grotesque?
2. Do you think the jury was manipulated by Wishman?

From CONFESSIONS OF A CRIMINAL LAWYER, by Seymour Wishman, Copyright
© 1981 by Seymour Wishman. Reprinted by permission of Times Books, a Division of Random House, Inc.

And so [I] began my career as a criminal defense lawyer. Starting a practice was exciting, but it brought a host of new anxieties. It became clear immediately that the practice of law was, among other things, a business like any other business, and I gradually learned how it ran. I had been nervous about whether I could get clients, but they came. Within a year I was working between sixty and seventy hours a week and earning a good living. And that workload had continued in the busy years that followed.

If I had asked myself what personal satisfaction I was deriving from the work, I could have said that there was ample satisfaction in defending people wrongly accused of a crime—except that very, very few of my clients had been *wrongly* accused. Since starting out, I had represented hundreds of people accused of crimes, and not only had most of them been guilty—many of them had been guilty of atrocities.

Pat Answers

Hundreds, I had represented hundreds—trying to keep them out of jail, keep them out on the street. I could no longer deflect the realization—this chilling glimpse of myself—that I had used all my skill and energy on behalf of a collection of criminals. Not all of them, but many, had been monsters—nothing less—who had done monstrous things. Sure, some of them might have been guilty of crimes made inevitable by poverty, but their victims hadn't caused their poverty, and most of the victims were equally poor. Furthermore, many people from backgrounds similar to my clients' didn't go out and mug or rape or kill.

For years non-lawyers had been asking me how I could defend such people. For years I had answered, like a trained lawyer, . . . that everyone was entitled to the best defense in order to make our system of justice work. Of course, that was true. But as I thought about my career . . . I asked myself why *I* should spend my life with these criminals? Most aspects of a law practice are less anxiety-ridden, more profitable, and more prestigious than criminal law.

I had to admit that I was getting more out of what I was doing as a criminal lawyer than money or the intellectual satisfaction of supporting the legal system. I would confess, over the years, to ego gratification and the joy of good craftsmanship: plotting out an intricate strategy, carrying off a good cross-examination, soaring through a moving summation—and the sound of a jury saying "not guilty"—are all thrilling. But why did I find it *so* thrilling? I knew, but only vaguely, that on a personal basis my courtroom performances also had something to do with a need for

189

power and control, respect and admiration. And as for any moral component to my work, I knew it had less to do with right and wrong than with an obscure identification with the underdog, even a despicable underdog, against authority.

The most disturbing question people often put to me—a question asked accusingly, over and over, but without touching me until now—was: "Don't you take responsibility for what a criminal you get off may do next?"

"Very little. About as much as a doctor who repairs the broken trigger finger of a killer," I used to answer flippantly.

I could no longer give that answer. . . .

Humiliating Victims To Get My Client Off

Weighing on me more heavily than the possibility that I had helped a guilty man escape punishment was the undeniable fact that I had humiliated the victim—alleged victim—in my cross-examination of her. But, as all criminal lawyers know, to be effective in court I had to act forcefully, even brutally, at times. I had been trained in law school to regard the "cross" as an art form. In the course of my career I had frequently discredited witnesses. My defense of myself had always been that there was nothing personal in what I was doing. This woman was obviously unwilling to dismiss my behavior as merely an aspect of my professional responsibility.

Seymour Wishman, *Confessions of a Criminal Lawyer*, 1981.

The jurors sat in their designated seats in the jury box. The clerk was in his chair in front and to the right of the judge's elevated desk. The court reporter was seated between the jury and the judge's desk. The D.A. stared straight ahead from his place ten feet away at the other end of counsel table. A court officer stood behind my client, and another court officer was leaning against the window looking out into the polluted air of downtown Newark; the window, the familiar institutional gun slit, was tall and narrow. Spectators filled the rows behind the wooden rail separating them from me in the well of the courtroom. The harsh fluorescent light glaring and humming down at us made the only sound in the room as we all waited for the judge to come out and resume the trial, now in its eighth day. The present trial had begun immediately after my distressing loss in Phil Lanza's case.

Assessing the Jurors

I looked over at my client, Richard Williams, seated next to me at counsel table. Legs crossed, his hands folded in his lap, he looked over at the jury, his dark brown eyes half closed, fixing on one juror at a time, studying the faces, probably trying to figure his chances with each juror, reaching some conclusion and moving

190

on to the next one. Some of the jurors were staring back. . . .

My mind drifted to my preoccupations of the last months—I wondered how many times I had been asked what I got out of being a criminal lawyer. "You spend most of your time with monsters," "You're in and out of depressing places like prisons all day long," "The pay isn't extraordinary," "You're looked down upon by judges, other lawyers, and the public." It wasn't hard to explain why very few lawyers did criminal work and even fewer went on doing it for any length of time. I struggled to understand why I had remained in this work for more than fifteen years. . . .

Using Emotion To Win

All . . . emotions and skills . . . were supposed to be deployed for one purpose—winning. During the cross-examination, all available energy was spent on beating the witness. With a tough witness, the duel could be dramatic. Only rarely, and with great reluctance, would a lawyer admit that more than the pleasure of good craftsmanship has been involved in his subduing of a witness, but I had seen lawyers work a witness over, control him, dominate and humiliate him, then torment him. Deriving enjoyment from inflicting that unnecessary measure of pain might be rare, but not that rare. If the witness was a woman, there might even be sexual overtones to the encounter. With some lawyers, perhaps sometimes with me, similar patterns could be played out in personal relationships.

I looked over at my client. Williams had lost a little weight during the eight months he had spent in jail. He looked a little less menacing, but his attitude was just as bloodless. It was upsetting to think I now had to be publicly associated with him, viewed as his ally, possibly his friend. But I still had the reflex of wanting to be a good lawyer. I worked to create the impression that I liked him. If the jury thought I found him hateful, they would be more likely to hate him, too.

I smiled at my client, acting solicitously toward him, pouring water for him from the decanter on counsel table into the little paper cup; I learned over and spoke gently, understandingly, with him. We sat at the end of counsel table together. I worked as hard as I could for him, using all my skill and energy on his behalf.

A Lower Form of Life

On the one hand, as I looked at this client, I often perceived him as some kind of lower form of life. But at the same time I identified with him. Like him, I felt myself to be an outsider, a loner. Some part of me had always remembered how frightened I has been during my Russian trial twenty years earlier: the anxiety of not knowing what was going to happen to you and having no control over events.

The judge opened the door of his chambers and entered the

courtroom. I placed my hand on my client's shoulder and held it firmly, reassuring him that I was with him, that we were in this together. I didn't look over to the jury, but I knew they were watching.

My client's wife, the mother of the child, took the witness stand. She had been charged with murder in the same indictment, but the D.A. had worked out an arrangement with her lawyer and agreed to dimiss her case in exchange for her testimony against my man. . . .

Guilty Clients' Lies

A criminal lawyer was surrounded by lies. Clients, witnesses, paid experts (such as psychiatrists), prosecutors—everybody—it seemed, lied or could be lying. Except me . . . most of the time . . . as far as I could tell. . . .

My initial response had been to overlook the fact that defendants lie, or, if I could not overlook it, to forgive them for it somehow. In a perverse way, I didn't feel it was as outrageous for them to lie as for other people. Defendants were desperately trying to stay out of prison, and I could sympathize with that desire after having spent so much time in prisons myself, as a visitor.

Seymour Wishman, *Confessions of a Criminal Lawyer*, 1981.

The mother described how my client had frequently beaten the child with a ferocity that on several occasions caused not only the infant but also the mother to become hysterical. When the child was eight months old, the father had beaten her so badly she'd had to be taken to the hospital and treated for a broken leg. As a result of that incident, a state agency took the child away from them for ten months. After returning Tanya, a social worker came by about once a month to ask how things were going. "Richard was home all the time. He couldn't get no job. And he seemed angrier and angrier. And when Tanya cried, it made him furious."

Using Photos To Shock

The D.A. walked over to his place at counsel table and removed a collection of eight-by-ten glossy photographs from a manila folder. He walked back to the witness and showed her the photographs of her two-year-old daugther lying naked on a slab, her little body scarred from whipping and cigarette burns, holes visible where pieces of flesh had been torn away.

I can still hear the mother's agonized wail.

It seemed incredible that both the D.A. and I had been surprised by the mother's reaction. I told him that had I still been pro-

192

secuting, I might have unwittingly presented the photographs just as he had. Too many years of atrocities had deadened our ability to respond to human tragedy. How the hell could we have been surprised that a mother would cry out when shown photographs of her mutilated daughter? . . .

Soliciting Sympathy from the Jury

No witnesses had been present when the girl died, except, perhaps—as the D.A. maintained—my client. I had to put him on the stand to explain, as no one else could, that he had disciplined his child earlier that day, but had been out of the kitchen when she apparently fell out of her chair, hitting her head on the tile floor and causing the fatal injury.

I also had to put the father on the stand to get him to belie the image of the cold, remorseless batterer depicted in the state's case. The jury had to be convinced he was human before they could believe he was innocent.

Through most of his testimony he spoke impassively, with a mean mask of a face. None of my questions prompted him to answer in a way that made him seem even remotely sympathetic. Finally, as a last resort, I surprised him with the same horrific morgue shots that had been shown to his wife.

"Did you do this to your own daughter?" I asked accusingly, sounding more like a prosecutor than his lawyer.

"Some of the marks. Yes. My wife also beat her."

"How could you do such a thing?"

"She kept crying. She'd mess in her pants, things like that. I had to teach her," he answered tentatively, taken back by my anger. "I thought that's what you're supposed to do."

From the far end of the jury box, holding the photographs for the jury to see, my voice charged with emotion, I screamed, "Did you love her?"

There was a long silence.

"Yes," he said softly, looking at the jury, "I loved her very much."

The jurors were looking at the photographs of the mutilated child, and, now, at last, heard barely restrained pain and remorse from my client. The male foreman wept.

It was very effective.

As I sat waiting to present my summation of my client's life, I came to some conclusions about my own. For years, . . . I'd had no difficulty separating myself from my clients, and even from aspects of my own behavior that I found distasteful. But although I had been unaware of the extent of my detachment, and, at times, had even taken pride in my ability to keep so many things from touching me, I had been paying a heavy price.

Yes, I'd had to adjust to the world I had been part of for so much of the last fifteen years. I had adjusted to the violence and the inhumanity. I had adjusted to the lies, the incompetence, and the brutality. . . .

The constant exposure to so many lies had made me suspicious of people. I had formed the habit of automatically sizing up character and trustworthiness, searching out motives. I had developed a reflex of recalling all inconsistent statements, no matter how trivial. These were good habits for a criminal lawyer—if only they hadn't bled into my personal life.

Destroying witnesses had led to an arrogance, to an inflated sense of control over people, that I found difficult, at times, to leave behind in the courtroom. The temptation to dominate a social situation or individual encounter was sometimes irresistible. This arrogance would betray itself in an impatience with people who were not speaking "relevantly" or "responsibly."

Even more dismaying, the need to function dispassionately had widened the distance between my emotional and my intellectual reactions. In this latest murder case, for which I was about to deliver a summation, I had been making a constant effort not to call the two-year-old daughter "it" in front of the jury—but "it" was what I was usually thinking. . . .

Screening Cases

I knew it would be a while before I would try another case. My career had taken an important turn. Of course I still believed everyone was entitled to the best defense, and entitled as well to a competent lawyer. But not necessarily to me.

I would have to screen my cases from now on. I had never turned down a case because the crime or the criminal were despicable—but now that would change. I could no longer cope with the ugliness and brutality that had for so long, too long, been a part of my life. . . .

The Summation

During the summation I felt I had to deal with the old scars of the wounds Williams had admitted inflicting on his child. Among other things I said:

> How much of the behavior in our lives can we really be held responsible and accountable for? It is with arrogance that we think of ourselves as free spirits, unfettered by unknown forces from our pasts. We would prefer to think of ourselves as having been born fully grown, without some invisible hand tugging strings tied to our limbs when we were too young to see what was happening to us. There are times for all of us when our so-called adult behavior is beyond our poor intelligence to comprehend.
>
> A father who has himself been battered and brutalized as an infant, may watch his own behavior toward his child in bewilderment and horror. He may see himself inflicting unnecessary pain on someone he loves without at all understanding that he is being driven by an unconscious memory. He may justify his

behavior by calling it discipline, or say that it is in the best interest of the child, but at a deeper level his striking out at someone he loves so dearly is irrational, and the harm he has done is not intentional. Somehow, by God's grace, most of us are able to restrain ourselves from the cruder ways of inflicting pain on those we love and on ourselves. But surely all of us, for reasons inexplicable to us, have hurt loved ones and ourselves. How much of our own behavior do we really understand? When this man accused of this most horrendous crime inflicted the wounds on his child which appear in the photographs as old scars, his hand was moved by pain lying beneath old scars of his own. We must weep for the dead child—for her death, and for the pain she had to endure while she lived. And we must weep with the thought that had she lived, she might very well have inflicted the same kind of pain on her own child, with the same bewilderment and horror that the defendant felt. We must pray that as human beings we may come to know ourselves better, and pray also that this increased self-knowledge may make a difference.

Of course, I am not saying that a person shouldn't be held responsible for his actions. What I am urging is that we bring some humility to our judgment of ourselves—and to our judgment of others, and that with greater compassion and generosity we struggle to understand their faults and our own.

After the summations the judge instructed the jury about the law to apply in deciding the case. When he had finished, the jury went into the jury room to deliberate. I decided to wait for the verdict on the wooden bench in the corridor outside the courtroom.

The Verdict

"Bring in the jury," the judge said, looking over in the direction of my client. Williams stared straight ahead, the flicker of emotion he had shown while testifying long since extinguished.

One by one the jurors walked out of the jury room, filed into the box, and took their seats. Their faces looked grim, which usually meant bad news for a defendant. They didn't look at the defendant, which was also likely to mean a convicton.

"Ladies and gentlemen of the jury," the judge said, "how say you through your foreman? Is the defendant, Richard Williams, guilty or not guilty of the charge?"

The foreman looked down at the piece of paper rattling in his shaking hand. I held my fountain pen in my hand, as I always did when listening for a verdict.

"Your Honor," the foreman spoke slowly, "we find the defendant not guilty of murder in the first degree, not guilty of murder in the second degree, and guilty of manslaughter."

Williams showed no sign of even hearing the decision about his fate. We were both drained of all energy. I leaned over to him. "Did you understand that?" I asked.

He gave a short nod.

"You'll probably get a sentence of six to eight years. You'll be eligible for parole after a third of the minimum. So with credit for good behavior and the time you've served waiting for trial, you'll be out in about a year," I said.

There was no reaction.

"Do you understand?"

He looked at me, his eyes like cold black stones. "I understand perfectly," he said in a slow, flat voice. "I got over."

"No," I said, feeling sad and exhausted, "you didn't get over. All you got was a short sentence in state prison. Your daughter is dead and you seem incapable of human feeling. It seems to me you didn't get such a good deal."

It was better not to reflect too long on the pain I was feeling over the fact . . . that my defense of Williams, for whom I still had hardly a trace of warm human feeling, had brought what could only be called a spectacular victory.

As I left the courthouse, several people congratulated me. I thanked them and went home.

"Advertising has had a positive effect on the public's perception of lawyers."

Lawyer Advertising Should Continue

Ronald M. Sharrow

The landmark case *Bates v. the State Bar of Arizona* ruled that lawyer advertising was permissible. The pros and cons of lawyer advertising continue to be debated, however. In the following viewpoint, Ronald M. Sharrow, an attorney in Baltimore, Maryland, argues that lawyer advertising has has a positive effect on the profession. Before advertising, he argues, the public had little, if any knowledge, of the practice of law. Now, largely because of advertising, this ignorance has changed and the public's perception of the legal profession has improved, Sharrow believes.

As you read, consider the following questions:

1. What, according to the author, were the original objections to lawyer advertising? Why does Sharrow believe that these objections are without merit?
2. What is the author's opinion of lawyers who oppose advertising?
3. How can lawyers take advantage of advertising, according to the author?

Ronald M. Sharrow, "Should Lawyers Advertise?" *Maryland Bar Journal*, April 1986. Reprinted with permission.

For 200 years, the workings of the law was shrouded in mystery, and protected by a code of silence that played life's drama on a darkened stage behind a closed curtain to an empty theater. In June 1977, the profession had reached its nadir so that nothing . . . could have further damaged the image of lawyers and the judicial system. After 200 years of silence, a commercial that tells people to seek legal advice if they have been injured in an accident is better than telling them nothing at all.

Despite the claims of the Chief Justice of the Supreme Court, who takes every opportunity to condemn lawyer advertising as "contributing to the low public standing of the profession," advertising has had a positive effect on the public's perception of lawyers.

Studies by the American Bar Association . . . have found that legal advertising has not turned off the public but instead has contributed to the profession's enhanced reputation in the community. One study, based on a 20-week television advertising campaign conducted by the ABA in 1983, found that less than five percent of a target audience in Illinois had negative comments about any lawyer advertising, and attitudes about lawyers actually improved with some. Interestingly, those viewers in the higher socio-economic strata of the group upgraded their opinions of lawyers even more than others viewing those commercials.

Original Objections Unfounded

All of the initial objections to lawyer advertising have been proved to be without merit. It was predicted that the Courts would be inundated with frivolous litigation . . . well, that hasn't happened. It was feared that lawyers would deceive and mislead the public . . . well, some might, most won't, and until now, none have. It was feared that inadequate rules to control advertising by the Bar would inevitably lead to outlandish and overreaching commercials . . . well, not so.

Indeed, many Bar leaders who vehemently condemned advertising as hucksterism, now admit that most of it is professionally and responsibly done. Thomas S. Johnson, a prominent member of an Illinois law firm and member of an ABA committee on the delivery of legal services, admits that his worst fears of the consequences . . . were unfounded, and that most of today's advertising "is dignified, non-misleading, effectively produced, and of high quality."

While the public is reacting favorably, the profession, which has the most to gain, is still expending its energy and resources to oppose and restrict lawyer advertising. We are members of a profession plagued with problems. Instead of wasting our resources condemning lawyers who advertise, we should attempt to convince Chief Justice Warren Burger that most lawyers who advertise are dedicated, competent, public spirited people who bring credit to the profession. His public criticism does more to discredit the profession and the judiciary than even the worst of legal commercials. The resources and power of the nation's "number one" jurist would be better directed toward the resolution of the more serious problems such as reducing law school admissions, limiting the number of admissions to the Bar, and weeding out incompetent and dishonest lawyers who have caused much of the bad publicity that has harmed the profession's image.

Lawyers who do not choose to advertise realize that their practices are not threatened by those who do. Instead, the commercials often prompt potential clients to call any lawyer, and thus bring more business to the profession as a whole. More people are availing themselves of legal services as a result of advertising. We have begun to remove the barrier that stood between the public and the profession by debunking some of the mystery. We have taken steps to inform the public about their legal rights.

More People Served

Whether advertising demeans the prestige of lawyers is far less significant than whether advertising has benefited the public.

Here the answer is resoundingly clear: Law firms that advertise are providing counseling to a far larger segment of the public at a far lower cost than has ever been done before by the legal profession.

Joel Hyatt, *USA Today*, July 10, 1985.

A 1984 report of the United States Department of Commerce stated that lawyers' gross income rose to $8 billion in 1983, a growth the report attributed in part to the eased restriction on lawyer advertising.

Although advertising is not the panacea for the profession's ills, it is a giant step in the right direction. Advertising cannot make a good lawyer out of a bad one, and it doesn't take long for the public to spot the difference. You can gift wrap garbage, but it is still garbage. Unless an attorney does an efficient and effective job for clients, all of the advertising and gift wrapping in the world won't help. Advertising might bring the clients to the door, but they won't stay if they perceive that he can not deliver.

Advertising is not for everyone. If all lawyers advertised, there would be no available television time for Proctor & Gamble. Only 13 percent of the nation's lawyers have ever advertised their services. But advertising is the best way of reaching the largest number of people. It isn't enough to be a lawyer representing the privileged few; the law belongs to everyone. A lawyer owes his dedication to the profession and the causes of the public. He must reach out, and one good way of doing so is through dignified and effective advertising.

Most of the criticism of the advertising that has been done since the *Bates* decision has come from lawyers who are not engaged in the private practice of law. The main thrust of this criticism seems to be that the advertisements are not educational enough, and that the advertising is being done for pecuniary gain by the lawyers who are advertising. Whether or not one wishes to accept the realities of a highly competitive nation, the practice of law is a business conducted for pecuniary gain. Any lawyer who spends his hard earned money to advertise for the sake of educating the public, without an eye toward pecuniary gain, is a fool soon parted with his money.

Educating the Public

The job of educating the public belongs to the organized Bar. . . . The American Bar Association has spent a great deal of its resources and money conducting studies, surveys, and writing reports, but has done little to educate the public. Since the studies reveal that the public reacts favorably to lawyer advertising and there has been an increase in the dollars spent for legal services, the organized Bar should pick up the challenge and conduct a nationwide educational campaign on television to create more business for the nation's lawyers and better inform the public instead of wasting its time and money on more studies and surveys. . . .

Advertising by lawyers is here to stay. Shouldn't we take advantage of this newly found power for the benefit of the public and the profession?

200

"Those who are concerned about the public image of our profession would do well to look at some of this shoddy advertising."

Lawyer Advertising Should Be Reevaluated

Edward F. Shea Jr.

Edward F. Shea Jr. is a partner in a Maryland law firm. In the following viewpoint, Shea argues that lawyer advertising has harmed the public's perception of lawyers. He believes that the legal profession is viewed by the public as one which should place ethical concerns above monetary gain. By advertising bargain basement divorces and such, lawyers undermine their professionalism.

As you read, consider the following questions:

1. What have been the traditional ways lawyers have found clients, according to Shea?
2. Why does the author believe advertising places an emphasis on lawyers' concern over money?
3. Do you think lawyers should be allowed to advertise their services? Why or why not?

Edward F. Shea Jr., "Should Lawyers Advertise?" *Maryland Bar Journal*, April 1986. Reprinted with permission.

President John F. Kennedy once observed that to become a statesman, a person first must be elected. Thus, we have politicians. Similarly, to practice law, an attorney first must acquire a client. The means to that goal should be befitting a profession associated with the administraion of justice.

Until recently, the methods available for building a law practice were limited. Some frequently-traveled paths included seeking political office or becoming involved in charitable or civic activities. By broadening contacts in the community, the attorney hoped potential clients would be duly impressed with his learning and wisdom. Then they would later refer legal matters to him. About the only other approved method of attracting clients was to succeed in each legal matter entrusted to the lawyer. For the traditionalist, each satisfied client was a certain source of more legal business. Of course, the novice lawyer still had to find that first client.

Nearly all other methods of seeking clients were deemed unethical. In fact, when I began practicing law in the 1950's, the firm with which I became associated did not permit its members to carry business cards. Such care to stay within the bounds of the Canons of Ethics was not unusual. . . .

We have seen a dramatic change in how the members of the legal profession seek clients. The telephone company's yellow pages are filled with advertisements, some as large as half a page, for lawyers of all specialties. Ads are also placed in newspapers and magazines while television seems to be favored by many attorneys.

It is time for the Bench and the Bar to look again into advertising by attorneys. What benefits, if any, has the public gained from lawyer advertising? More importantly, what has advertising done for the legal profession? Has it improved the administration of justice, increased respect for the legal profession or provided improved legal representation for our citizens?

Shoddy Advertising

In the January 1985 issue of the *ABA Journal,* Chief Justice Warren E. Burger said, "Those who are concerned about the public image of our profession would do well to look at some of this shoddy advertising. It is not just unprofessional; it is anti-professional. I particularly would point to some of the newspaper ads such as, 'For a limited period, uncontested divorces for $199.95.' Or as has happened, ads including a coupon worth $10 or $15 for the first interview, as though clients were going to a supermarket to buy groceries."

In some legal circles, the Chief Justice is viewed as somewhere to the right to Louis XIV, but those attorneys who believe that the law is first of all a learned profession and only secondly an occupation applaud the Chief Justice's dedication to upholding the highest ideals for lawyers. In the . . . case of *Zauderer v. Office of Disciplinary Counsel,* (1985) Justice Sandra D. O'Connor put it this way in an opinion: "The States understandably require more of attorneys than of others engaged in commerce. Lawyers are professionals, and as such they have greater obligations. As Justice Frankfurter once observed, '[f]rom a profession charged with

[constitutional] responsibilities there must be exacted . . . qualities of truth-speaking, of a high sense of honor, of granite discretion.' The legal profession has in the past been distinguished and well served by a code of ethics which imposes certain standards beyond those prevailing in the marketplace and by a duty to place professional responsibility above pecuniary gain.''. . .

Former ABA President Leonard S. Janofsky delivered an address entitled "Is the S in Esquire Becoming a $ Sign?'' Janofsky wisely observed: "When lawyers treat the system of justice as a game designed to fatten their pocketbooks, the whole system is debased. The public's confidence in the law diminishes and our democracy is weakened.''

Following the *Bates* decision, [permitting lawyer advertising] the Maryland Court of Appeals adopted amendments . . . to permit advertising by attorneys. Two of the judges, Chief Judge Robert C. Murphy and Judge Harry A. Cole did not concur in the adoption of the new rules. In his statement appended to the Rules Order, Chief Judge Murphy objected to the Court's rejection of the recommendation of the Standing Committee on Rules calling for seven additional subsections. Those subsections, which had the support of the Maryland State Bar Association . . . , would have provided guidelines regarding fee and quality advertising. The two dissenting judges deemed the additional provisions as "essential to meaningful and effective regulation of lawyer advertising.''

Judge Murphy warned: "Not to adopt the additional subsections . . . is to make no distinction between the advertising of legal service and the advertising of consumer products.'' If the Court of Appeals were to review some of the current advertising it might be difficult for the judges to distinguish those for legal services from those for consumer products.

Destroying the Professional Ideal

After the adoption of the amendments, . . . the views of several attorneys on the question of advertising were published. George W. Liebmann, of the Baltimore City Bar Association, speculated on what the future holds. "Consumer benefit is the benefit on which the courts have focused,'' said Liebmann. "The detriment is to a professional ideal, also founded on client interests; one frequently honored in the breach, but not hitherto the object of cheap cynicism by high courts—that professional competition should take place on the basis of reputation with clients and fellow practitioners and that a professional relationship rests on a sounder basis when initiated by the client and not the lawyer. The radiations of the decisions in this sphere may extend to such matters as how the profession and not merely its few advertising members is perceived, how and by whom it is regulated, what personal attributes induce professional success, what sorts of younger people are drawn to enter the profession, and what sorts of offices and practices shape their rise to professional maturity."

After the experience of recent years, the time is appropriate for the organized Bar to engage in a study of the effects upon the profession that have come from advertising. Has respect for the law and the lawyer improved? Have lawyers developed a deeper sense of responsibility to their clients and the administration of justice? What of the young people engaged in the study of law? Do they see the profession as a vocation engaged in the highest calling or solely as a lucrative occupation leading to fame and fortune? Janofsky says, "Of course, lawyers have a right to earn a living, a right to charge a fee and even a right to advertise our services, but before any right, we have an obligation. That our obligation comes first is what makes us professionals."

As professionals then, let us reexamine the advertising of legal services.

Distinguishing Between Fact and Opinion

This activity is designed to help develop the critical thinking skill of distinguishing between fact and opinion. Consider the following statement as an example: "The government has the burden of proving, beyond a reasonable doubt, that the citizen accused is guilty of each and every element of the offense." This statement is a fact about a goal of the American justice system. But consider another statement: "In seducing clients to purchase their wares, lawyers too often, too closely, resemble those who service the public in the one profession that pre-dates the legal trade." This statement clearly is an expressed opinion about the way lawyers seek clients.

When investigating controversial issues it is important that one be able to distinguish between statements of fact and statements of opinion. It is also important to recognize that not all statements of fact are true. They may appear to be true, but some are based on inaccurate or false information. For this activity, however, we are concerned with understanding the difference between those statements which appear to be factual and those which appear to be based primarily on opinion.

The following statements are taken from the viewpoints in this chapter. Consider each statement carefully. *Mark O for any statement you believe is an opinion or interpretation of facts. Mark F for any statement you believe is a fact. Mark I for any statement you believe is impossible to judge.*

If you are doing this activity as a member of a class or group, compare your answers with those of other class or group members. Be able to defend your answers. You may discover that others will come to different conclusions than you. Listening to the reasons others present for their answers may give you valuable insights in distinguishing between fact and opinion.

If you are reading this book alone, ask others if they agree with your answers. You too will find this interaction valuable.

O = *opinion*
F = *fact*
I = *impossible to judge*

1. The constant exposure to so many lies can make a lawyer suspicious of people.

2. The practice of law is a business like any other business.

3. Judges like it when the best lawyering wins.

4. Many criminal lawyers are looked down upon by judges, other lawyers, and the public.

5. The courtroom scene and the lawyer as hero or villain are high points of television and the movies.

6. Ultimately, lawyers must seek, as their goal and satisfaction not love of being loved, but love of law.

7. Human tragedy routinely provides the setting for the work of lawyers.

8. Lawyers seem to be well on their way to accomplishing the proverbial impossible—that one can get rich doing good.

9. Judges have the discretion to reduce jury awards.

10. In the past, the methods available to lawyers for attracting clients were limited.

11. The advertising of legal services is unprofessional and anti-professional.

12. More professionalism is required of attorneys than of others engaged in business.

13. The legal profession has a duty to place professional responsibility above pecuniary gain.

14. Lawyers have a right to advertise their services.

15. A study conducted by the ABA found that less than five percent of a target audience had negative comments about any lawyer advertising.

16. More people are availing themselves of legal services as a result of advertising.

17. Advertising is a dignified and effective way for a lawyer to reach out to the public.

Periodical Bibliography

The following list of periodical articles deals with the subject matter of this chapter.

Peter Megargee Brown — "Misguided Lawyers," *The New York Times,* December 6, 1983.

Roy Cohn — "Is Justice for Everyone?" *Parade Magazine,* April 22, 1984.

J.R. Elkins — "Ethics: Professionalism, Craft and Failure," *Kentucky Law Journal,* 1984/1985.

Florida Bar Journal — "Marketing Legal Services the Professional Way," February 1985.

Kirkland Grant — "The Wrong Way To Pursue Lawyer Incompetency," *American Bar Association Journal,* September 1983.

Mark Guralnick — "Someone Has To Defend the Drug Dealers," *Student Lawyer,* February 1984.

Sharon Johnson — "A Plague of Lawyers," *Working Woman,* September 1984.

Irving R. Kaufman — "Attorney Incompetence: A Plea for Reform," *American Bar Association Journal,* March 1983.

J.L. Kirsch — "War on Lawyers? Criminal Defense Lawyers Claim They Have Become Open Targets in the Federal Prosecutors' War on Crime," *California Lawyer,* March 1985.

Loyola University at Chicago Law Journal — "Direct Mailings by Attorneys: Which End of the Spectrum?" Spring 1985.

Richard Pollack — "The Epilepsy Defense," *The Atlantic Monthly,* May 1984.

J.M. Reisman — "The Whole Truth and Nothing But the Truth: Is the Trier of Fact Entitled To Hear It?" *University of Richmond Law Review,* Spring 1985.

Mark E. Rust — "Volunteer Lawyers Working for the Poor Don't Always Have What It Takes To Help," *Student Lawyer,* May 1985.

Robert J. Samuelson — "The Lawyering of America," *Newsweek,* March 10, 1986.

TRB from Washington — "Liars and Lawyers," *The New Republic,* December 16, 1985.

Organizations To Contact

The editors have compiled the following list of organizations which are concerned with the issues debated in this book. All of them have publications or information available for interested readers. The descriptions are derived from materials provided by the organizations.

American Civil Liberties Union (ACLU)
22 E. 40th St.
New York, NY 10016
(212) 944-9800

The ACLU is one of America's oldest civil liberties organizations. Founded in 1920, the ACLU champions the rights set forth in the Declaration of Independence and the Constitution. The Foundation of the ACLU provides legal defense, research, and education. It publishes the quarterly newspaper *Civil Liberties* and various pamphlets, books, and position papers.

American Judicature Society
200 W. Monroe St., Suite 1606
Chicago, IL 60606
(312) 558-6900

A group of lawyers, judges, law teachers, government officials, and citizens interested in effective administration of justice. The society conducts research, offers a consultation service, and works to combat court congestion and delay. Publishes *Judicature.*

Americans for Effective Law Enforcement (AELE)
5519 N. Cumberland Ave., #1008
Chicago, IL 60656
(312) 763-2800

AELE attempts to help police, prosecutors, and the courts promote fairer, more effective administration of criminal law and equal justice for all. Publications include a monthly bulletin and several other regular publications.

Center for Constitutional Rights
853 Broadway, Suite 1401
New York, NY 10003
(212) 674-3303

The Center works to halt and reverse the steady erosion of civil liberties in the US. Publishes a variety of public information.

Center for Law in the Public Interest
10951 W. Pico Blvd., 3rd Floor
Los Angeles, CA 90064
(213) 470-3000

A group of attorneys who represent groups without charge and litigate class action cases. Publishes a quarterly newsletter.

Citizens in Defense of Civil Liberties (CDCL)
343 S. Dearborn St., #918
Chicago, IL 60604

CDCL works to defend civil liberties through educational programs and publications. Publishes several quarterly newsletters, books, and other information.

Committee for Equality of Citizens Before the Courts (CO-EQUAL)
2762 N. Clybourn Ave.
Chicago, IL 60614
(312) 549-8070

CO-EQUAL is interested in protecting and advancing due process of law in both civil and criminal proceedings. The group publishes a newsletter and monographs.

HALT: Americans for Legal Reform
201 Massachusetts Ave. NE, Suite 319
Washington, DC 20002
(202) 546-4258

The organization seeks to relieve the average citizen of the oppressive cost of a lawyer and the lengthy procedural entanglements of litigation. HALT believes that many transactions can be handled with minimal or no lawyer intervention.

National Association for Crime Victims Rights
PO Box 16161
Portland, OR 97216
(503) 252-9012

Association members are local businesses, professional groups, and others "fed up" with the increase in crime. Through Operation Strike Back, it attempts to show people that there is an alternative to living in fear of crime. It publishes a bimonthly newsletter.

National Association of Criminal Defense Lawyers
1815 H St. NW, Suite 550
Washington, DC 20006
(202) 872-8688

An association of lawyers interested in the defense of individuals charged with crime. Publishes a magazine ten times a year.

National Chamber Litigation Center (NCLC)
1615 H St. NW
Washington, DC 20062

NCLC views litigation as a means to curb the influence of government regulations on business. The Center works to overturn laws, regulations, and court rulings which violate businesses' constitutional rights and legal interests. Publishes a quarterly newsletter.

National Criminal Justice Association
444 N. Capitol St. NW, Suite 608
Washington, DC 20001
(202) 347-4900

Provides a forum for development and expression of unified state views on criminal and juvenile justice issues. Its objectives are to focus attention on controlling crime and improving individual states' administration of their criminal and juvenile justice systems.

National Institute of Victimology
2333 N. Vernon St.
Arlington, VA 22207
(703) 528-8872

Founded in 1976, the Institute works to improve **victim/witness** services and to make the public and criminal justice personnel aware of the needs of crime victims. Publishes *Victimology: An International Journal*.

National Organization for Victim Assistance
717 D St. NW
Washington, DC 20531
(202) 393-6682

Serves as a national forum for victim advocacy by providing direct services to victims of crime where no services exist, providing education and technical assistance to service providers on victim issues, and serving as a membership organization for those who support the victims' movement.

Trial Lawyers for Public Justice (TLPJ)
2000 P St. NW, Suite 611
Washington, DC 20036
(202) 463-8600

TLPJ works to bring damage lawsuits against corporations and governments on health, safety, and other regulatory issues. Publishes several newsletters regarding its cases.

VERA Institute of Justice
30 E. 39th St.
New York, NY 10016
(212) 986-6910

VERA conducts action-research projects in criminal justice reform. The Institute's projects include the Manhattan Bail Project, which made recommendations to the court, and the Victim/Witness Assistance Project which provides services to victims and civilian police prosecution witnesses.

Victims for Victims
1800 S. Robertson Blvd., Suite 400
Los Angeles, CA 90036
(213) 850-5001

The group's purpose is to help victims of violent crime deal with the physical and psychological damage and to promote victims' rights. Publishes a newsletter and various brochures.

Victims of Crime and Leniency
PO Box 1283
114 N. Hull St.
Montgomery, AL 36103
(205) 261-4010

An organization of individuals who have been victims of crime, the group seeks to ensure that crime victims' rights are recognized and protected. They believe that the US justice system goes to great lengths to protect the rights of criminals while discounting those of victims. Publishes a quarterly newsletter.

Bibliography of Books

Jerold S. Auerbach — *Justice Without Law?* New York: Oxford University Press, 1983.

Stephen Brophy — *Crime, Justice and Morals.* Boston: Routledge Kegan Paul, 1984.

Frank Carrington — *Crime and Justice: A Conservative Strategy.* Washington, DC: Heritage Foundation, 1983.

Michael Castleman — *Crime Free: Stop Your Chances of Being Robbed, Raped, Mugged or Burglarized.* New York: Simon & Schuster, 1984.

Elliott Currie — *Confronting Crime.* New York: Pantheon Books, 1985.

Malcolm M. Feeley — *Court Reform on Trial.* New York: Basic Books, 1983.

Lois G. Forer — *Criminals & Victims.* New York: W.W. Norton, 1980.

James F. Gilginan — *Doing Justice: How the System Works, as Seen by the Participants.* Englewood Cliffs, NJ: Prentice-Hall, 1982.

Stephen Goode — *The Controversial Court.* New York: Julian Messner, 1982.

Bertram Harnett — *Law, Lawyers and Laymen.* San Diego: Harcourt Brace Jovanovich, 1984.

Daryl A. Hellman — *The Economics of Crime.* New York: St. Martin's Press, 1980.

Bruce Jackson — *Law and Disorder: Criminal Justice in America.* Bloomington: University of Indiana Press, 1985.

Philip J. Jenkins — *Crime and Justice: Issues and Ideas.* Monterey, CA: Brooks-Cole, 1984.

Don B. Kates Jr. — *Firearms and Violence.* San Francisco: Pacific Institute for Public Policy Research, 1984.

Gary Kinder — *Victim: The Other Side of Murder.* New York: Delacorte Press, 1982.

Jethro K. Lieberman — *The Litigious Society.* New York: Basic Books, 1981.

David Luban, ed. — *The Good Lawyer: Lawyers' Roles and Lawyers' Ethics.* Totowa, NJ: Rowman & Allanheld, 1983.

Richard Neely — *Why Courts Don't Work.* New York: McGraw-Hill, 1983.

Richard A. Posner — *The Federal Courts: Crisis and Reform.* Cambridge, MA: Harvard University Press, 1985.

Jeffrey H. Reiman — *The Rich Get Richer and the Poor Get Prison: Ideology, Class and Criminal Justice.* New York: John Wiley & Sons, 1984.

Stanley E. Rosenblatt — *Trial Lawyer.* Secaucus, NJ: Lyle Stuart, 1984.

Jeffrey Leigh Sedgwick — *Deterring Criminals.* Washington, DC: American Enterprise Institute, 1980.

Philip M. Stern — *Lawyers on Trial.* New York: Times Books, 1980.

Ann Strick — *Injustice for All: How Our Adversary System of Law Victimizes Us and Subverts True Justice.* New York: Penguin Books, 1978.

Eugene D. Wheeler and Robert E. Kallman	*Stop Justice Abuse.* Ventura, CA: Pathfinder Press, 1986.
James Q. Wilson	*Thinking About Crime.* New York: Basic Books, 1983.
James Q. Wilson and Richard J. Herrnstein	*Crime and Human Nature.* New York: Simon and Schuster, 1985.
Seymour Wishman	*Anatomy of a Jury.* New York: Times Books, 1986.

Index

accused
 and *Miranda*
  as necessary, 114-121
  as unnecessary, 122-129
 rights of
  as excessive, 102-107
  as ineffective, 108-113
Adler, Norman A., 63
adversary system
 as cause of injustice, 51-56
 need for, 45-50
Alexander, Ken, 92
American Psychological Association
 report on crime victims, 136-137,
 138

Babcock, Barbara Allen, 183
Bard, Morton, 154
Berry, Jim, 136
Brakel, Samuel Jan, 173
Braden, Tom, 95
Brink, David R., 170
Brookes, Warren T., 35
Burger, Warren E., 102, 199, 202-203

Clark, Kenneth B., 28
Cleary, John J., 142, 152
Cohn, Roy, 112
Conine, Ernest, 86
Cooley, John W., 77
courts
 are to blame for crime, 35, 36
 need to protect accused, 41, 43-44
crime
 causes of
  moral disintegration, 34
  social, 17, 24-32
   as myth, 18
  unemployment, 28
 definition of, 26-27
crime prevention, 17, 19
crime rate
 as soaring, 35-36
 statistics, 103, 144
crime victims, *see* victims
criminal justice system
 as criminal, 25-26, 27, 31-32
 as favoring offenders, 33-34, 39
 as unfair to poor, 24-32
 criminals as victims of, 29-32
 flaws in, 22-23
 need to protect the accused, 40
 purpose of
  deterrence, 19-20, 104-105

punishment, 16-23, 37
 suggestions to improve, 38-39
 unfair to poor, 110-113
criminals
 as innocent victims, 31-32
  myth of, 23, 34
 need to condemn, 19-21
  as wrong, 25
 need to punish, 37
 recidivism of, 36, 106
 relish crime, 18-19
 rights of
  as undermining justice, 36, 189
  need to modify, 35

Daniels, Stephen, 79
Darrow, Clarence, 181, 187
DiPerna, Paula, 59, 61

Forer, Lois G., 84, 97, 108
Freedman, Monroe, 53

Gamble, Ed, 88
Gibb, Tom, 75
Goetz, Bernhard Hugo, 163
Gould, Charles L., 33
gun control laws, 165

Harnett, Bertram, 40
Heilman, John, 73
Heinz, John, 143
Henderson, Lynne N., 150
Hyatt, Joel, 199

judges
 as alternative to jury, 60-61
 criticisms of, 58-59
  as unfair, 42-43
jury system
 alternatives to
  as inadequate, 58
 and civil courts, 83-84
 as working, 57-62
 need to reform, 63-67

Kamisar, Yale, 116
Kelley, Steve, 147, 160
Kennedy, John F., 202
Kinsley, Michael, 90
Kunen, James S., 179

Landsman, Stephan, 45
lawyer advertising
 as positive, 197-200